How Dare You Judge Us, God

Clifford Goldstein

Pacific Press Publishing Association
Boise, Idaho
Oshawa, Ontario, Canada

Edited by Lincoln E. Steed
Designed by Tim Larson
Cover by Lynn Bernasconi
Typeset in 10/12 Century Schoolbook

Copyright © 1991 by
Pacific Press Publishing Association
Printed in United States of America
All Rights Reserved

The author assumes full responsibility for the accuracy
of all facts and quotations cited in this book.

Library of Congress Catalog Card Number: 90-62283

ISBN 0-8163-0961-2

91 92 93 94 95 • 5 4 3 2 1

Contents

*S*pit out of their graves, billions of the world's dead assemble into a quivering sweep of flesh that wraps around the horizon and disappears. *Sumerian generals, Celtic merchants, Tibetan mystics, Colombian peasants, Wall Street skeptics—an immeasurable mass, almost all who have ever lived upon the earth, rise together, resurrected. The great judgment day has come, and unredeemed humanity stands before the bar of heaven. The crime: high treason against the Law of God. The verdict: guilty as charged. The sentence: eternal destruction.*

The condemned don't accept the decree lightly. Cries, curses, accusations surge from their lips, and they rage like an insane sea of boiling flesh.

"How dare You judge me, God!" a man with cropped blond hair shouts, raising a red fist. "What do You know about suffering? What do You know about pain?"

"Sure, I stole," another declares, "but I was hungry. What do You know about hunger, God?"

In the midst of the madness, a woman with painted eyes, a purple tear dripping down her cheek, is thrust on the shoulders of men who greedily handle her.

"What do You know about lust, God?" she accuses. "What do You know about temptation and passion? And yet You are going to sit in heaven and condemn me. We can't stop You! We can't escape, but we reject Your verdict, we reject Your sentence, and we reject You!"

They stomp feet and shake fists as waves of anger rise in hot currents, carrying their cries skyward: "HYPOCRITE! UNFAIR! HOW EASY IT IS TO BE GOOD IN HEAVEN! HOW DARE YOU JUDGE US!"

A Chinese man, dressed in black, drops his shirt and exposes a back gashed with deep gray scars. He says nothing, then straightens up and shakes a fist over his head while those in the crowd point to his scars and roar: "HOW DARE YOU JUDGE US, GOD!"

"I was arrested unjustly," another man, stepping forward, barks. "I was jailed, beaten, executed. And now, from the comfort of heaven, You condemn me to death—again?"

Amid the madness, each one defies God's right to judge them. A Jew shows the burns on his face from the Zyklon B in a Nazi gas chamber. A Black exposes the scars on his wrists from weeks in chains on a slave ship. Others, rejected by their own society, question whether God, who never knew the pain of rejection, has the right to judge those who have. Political prisoners, who had spoken out for freedom, for truth, and who stood up against tyranny at the cost of their lives, deny God the prerogative to judge them. Though each complaint is different, the consistent cry of this macabre chorus is: "HOW DARE YOU JUDGE US, GOD!"

CHAPTER One

Christina and the Bag Lady

While AIDS gobbles up swaths of Uganda, bites chunks out of homosexuals, and nibbles on straights, another disease devours all humanity. Rich or poor, young or old, religious or ir-religious, no one escapes. Most suffer quietly, their smiles hiding the cries within, though sorrow eventually bursts from all lips. Some just cry louder, and longer, than others.

The symptoms can vary, flux, they often do—yet the disease remains, stubborn as life. It sits, herpeslike, silent, concealed, awaiting only the right circumstances, and then it strikes, blistering the soul. The pain comes on gradually, or all at once.

To find relief, people stuff various solids (cocaine), liquids (alcohol), and gases (pot smoke) into their noses, bellies, and lungs—substances that can no more cure the problem than sex does syphilis. Others search the world, seeking counsel from medical doctors to witch doctors, from priests to shamans, but all in vain. Billions of dollars are squandered on books, seminars, retreats, chants, remedies that give, at most, only temporary respite.

The sickness itself isn't fatal, but many suffer so badly that they prefer death, even a painful one, than to battle. Most people, when severely stricken themselves, have questioned whether the struggle was worth it.

"Life," Abraham Cowley wrote, "is an incurable disease."

He's wrong. Life's not incurable, the dead prove that; nor is it a disease, no matter how sick it seems. The problem is not life, but the misery that mars it. Man's unhappiness, that's the disease, and we haven't been able to cure it, no matter how many millennia we've tried.

"Twins even from birth," wrote Homer over two thousand years ago, "are misery and man." Manhattan taxi driver Jose Martinez expressed the same idea in more prosaic terms.

We're here to die, just live and die. I drive a cab. I do some fishing, take my girl out, pay taxes, do a little reading, then get ready to drop dead. Life's a big fake. You're like the wind. After you're gone, other people will come. We're gonna destroy ourselves, nothing we can do about it. The only cure for the world's illness is nuclear war—wipe everything out and start over.

At birth, first facing life, we let out a cry; later, facing death, we often do the same. We cry at birth, perhaps, afraid of what's next; we cry at death, perhaps, because we don't know. Either way, between the first and last tear, we live an existence that, while peppered with moments of joy and happiness (the exceptions to prove the rule), is mostly pain, bitterness, and disappointment for most human flesh.

We see the homeless, their cracked and dirty palms cupped like dead cats, their eyes glazed with the disconnected stare of those who have seen things that would make demons quiver. About 500 homeless freeze to death every winter in the United States alone. Next time a bitter wind blunts against your door, imagine this same icy surge, resharpened, knifing into knotted flesh coiled on a bench, and marrow cold as snow.

Early one summer evening in Manhattan, as the local gliterati *wander into exclusive watering holes before appearing at the club or the show, a toothless bag lady, face folded in wrinkles, scrounges through a wire garbage can. Finding leftovers from McDonald's, she leans over the can and eats, her sunken lips quivering around a chicken bone. Amid mountains of glass and steel opulence, the sight of this old woman eating fowl out of the garbage wrestles me to a stop.*

"Are you really eating out of the garbage?" I ask.

She nods, sensing a sucker.

I stare, astonished. Then, in a gesture of defiance against a system that allows an elderly woman to eat like a dog, in a gesture of pity for a degraded old lady, but mostly in a gesture of desperation, I pull out my wallet, hand her ten dollars, and step back.

"Buy food," I plead. "Don't eat out of the garbage anymore. Do you promise to get food?"

She nods again, smiles toothlessly, and then disappears amid the neon and the gold, probably to buy a few bottles of MD 20-20.

Of course, misery doesn't proliferate only in rags, garbage cans, and alleys; it spreads among mink, diner's clubs, and mansions too. The rich, the famous, the beautiful suffer as do the poor, the unknown, and the ugly. Despite having what the rest of us dupes think would make us happy, the rich find that their silks, diamonds, and tinted-glass limos no more protect them from misery than a cardboard box protects a derelict from a blizzard.

Her yachts, even private islands in the Aegean, couldn't keep Christina Onassis from attempting suicide. Betty Ford drank herself into therapy, as did Kitty Dukakis, who declared, "I am an alcoholic." Elizabeth Taylor struggled with fat and booze and seven marriages. Frank Sinatra, doing it his way, tried to do himself in. Literary giant Truman Capote declared, "I drink because it is the only time I can stand it." Elvis Presley, racked with drugs, died at the foot of his toilet, his pajama bottoms around his ankles. Just before death, Pablo Picasso painted a self-portrait of a demented, tormented soul. Nobel prize winner Ernest Hemingway put a shotgun in his mouth and blew off his head.

Most of us, though, exist somewhere between Christina Onassis and the bag lady. Yet no matter if we hover within the gleam of Christina's jewels, or the stench of the bag lady's stockings, we all know pain, suffering, and disappointment; not because we read it in tabloids, or hear it in whispered rumor, or see it coiled on park benches—but because we experience it ourselves. Our own hearts bear the greatest witness, the most irrefutable evidence of our unhappiness.

"The mass of men," wrote Thoreau, "lead lives of quiet desperation."

How quiet, how desperate, it varies, but all—no matter how quiet—have been desperate. Men do snatch hints of happiness, but those are often as fleeting as a breeze. A newborn baby brings tears of joy to the mother, but how many more tears of bitterness and sorrow will she spill over that same child? Love brings bliss, but that love often turns to hate, the bliss to misery. If the intensity of emotion could be graphed, whose line would stretch longest on the chart: the couples in New York City who together spent $806,000 on marriage licenses in 1985, or those who that year in the same city spent $3,637,095 on divorce fees? We graph rape, but who measures the rage? We chart divorce, disease, and infant mortality, but lines, dots, and figures can no more depict the pain than a hoarse whisper can reproduce Beethoven's Ninth Symphony.

"Who breathes must suffer, and who thinks must mourn," wrote Matthew Prior, "and he alone is blessed who ne'er was born."

We dream, but our dreams are rarely fulfilled. In *Of Mice and Men*, novelist John Steinbeck wrote of George and Lennie, itinerant farmworkers during the Depression who had humble hopes: a small plot of land with a few animals, that's all. Yet Lennie, with a flimsy mind that couldn't control his hard muscles, accidently killed a woman, and frenzied avengers stalked them through the woods. George, wanting to spare his best friend from the rage of a lynch mob, stood behind Lennie, who—sitting along a river bank—didn't see the gun in George's hand.

George raised the gun and his hand shook, and he dropped his hand to the ground again.

"Go on," said Lennie. "How's it gonna be. We gonna get a little place."

"We'll have a cow," said George. "An' we'll have maybe a pig an' chickens . . . an' down the flat we'll have a . . . little piece of alfalfa—"

"For the rabbits," Lennie shouted.

"For the rabbits," George repeated.

"And I get to tend the rabbits."

"An' you'll get to tend the rabbits."

Lennie giggled with happiness. "An' live on the fatta the lan'."

"Yes."

Lennie turned his head.

"No, Lennie. Look down there acrost the river,

11

like you can almost see the place."

Lennie obeyed him. George looked down at the gun.

There were crashing footsteps in the brush now. George turned and looked toward them.

"Go on, George. When we gonna do it?"

"Gonna do it soon."

"Me an' you."

"You . . . an' me. Ever'body gonna be nice to you. Ain't gonna be no more trouble. Nobody gonna hurt nobody nor steal from 'em."

Lennie said, "I thought you was mad at me, George."

Then, just as the mob approached, George pulled the trigger.

Others struggle their whole lives, even sell their souls, for what they think will make them happy, yet for the few who get what they want, happiness rarely follows. King Solomon, the wealthiest man of antiquity, moaned, "I have seen all the works that are done under the sun; and behold, all is vanity and vexation of spirit" (Ecclesiastes 1:14). Today, 5 percent of Americans earning less than $15,000 a year say they have achieved the American dream; yet the percentage of those earning more than $50,000 a year who say the same thing is only one percent higher! Apparently, happiness is more than kingdom or a BMW.

No matter our fame, our success, or our accomplishments, we all struggle with secret little evils that lurk within. Even if we keep them capped in a dark, unused corner of the soul, we still hear their growls, feel their claws, and life can become nothing but a struggle to keep these vicious little creatures caged.

Why are our lives often like books in which, when we come to the final pages, we realize that it's not the story we wanted written? Why is it that the more self-absorbed we are, and the more we strive to gain for ourselves, the unhappier our lives? Why are we such wretches that often our happiest moments arise when we hear about someone else's misery? Why must "each one of us . . . suffer long to himself before he can learn that he is but one in a great community of wretchedness which has been pitilessly repeating itself from the foundation of the world" (William Dean Howells)?

One solution is easy. If we believe that "we are here because one odd group of fishes had a peculiar fin anatomy that could transform into legs for terrestrial creatures" (paleontologist Stephen Jay Gould), then we have an answer of sorts. If evolution explains us, then we are the products of luck—bad luck at that—and nothing more. As the unfortunate winners of some comic lottery that has stranded us on a blob of hardened lava in the middle of a cold, dead universe, we evolved amid a harsh and bitter struggle against the elements. Our essence, our existence, is rooted in nothing but chance. Sometimes the dice roll in our favor, sometimes not, but the odds for happiness are obviously against us. We live only because we happen to live, we suffer only because we happen to suffer, and it all has no more significance than do the numbers of a random throw of red-and-white dice on a blackjack table.

Many people, however, can't accept the cosmic-dice theory. They see in creation evidence that we are more than creatures of chance. By its complexity alone, human existence declares that we began from something more profound than blind luck in a slime pit. Edward Argyle, a Canadian scientist, estimated that the maximum number of bits of information that interacting chemicals can produce by sheer chance is 200. He calculated, too, that it requires about 6 million bits of information to produce a single-celled organism, about

13

240 million bits to make a man. By Argyle's reckoning at least, we are here by more than luck, good or bad. Francis Crick (of Crick and Watson fame) has written that DNA alone (not counting the rest of a cell) is just too complicated to have evolved unassisted in a mere 3.8 billion years (his estimate of the earth's age). Crick has recently touted a theory of panspermia, the idea that life, beginning somewhere else in the universe, was somehow brought to seed here.

Of course, some people—without a scientific background—have believed in a type of "panspermia" for thousands of years. Those who say that God created the world adhere to this same basic concept: the idea that life on earth originally comes from somewhere else in the universe. "But ask now the beasts, and they shall teach thee; and the fowls of the air, and they shall tell thee: Or speak to the earth, and it shall teach thee; and the fishes of the sea shall declare unto thee. Who knoweth not in all these that the hand of the Lord hath wrought this? In whose hand is the soul of every living thing, and the breath of all mankind" (Job 12:7-10).

Yet the notion of God, at least in the context of suffering, can be more disturbing than evolution. If we accept evolution, then at least we know that we can't passively read the meaning of life from what surrounds us, or even what preceded us, because no meaning exists there. If creation is an accident, then we are all accidents as well, and our lives therefore have no more inherent meaning than does the configuration of shattered glass left over from a car wreck. We can read something—anything we want, actually—into the debris, but the meaning becomes purely personal. "Man is nothing else," wrote existentialist godfather Jean-Paul Satre, "but what he makes of himself." Life, and its purpose, becomes as subjective as a hallucination.

Human pain, in this context at least, becomes more

understandable: we suffer because by sheer chance we have evolved in an amoral universe on a planet where odds are that we suffer. The idea of going around in endless circles surrounded only by the vacuous silence of the universe is not the most comforting thought, but at least suffering then makes more sense than it does if we believe in a Creator who supposedly loves His Creation.

How, for instance, do believers in God reconcile the idea of a loving God with the tens of thousands dead from the Armenian earthquake? Who dares, while millions starve, to proclaim that God is love? It's like saying to someone, "I love you," while abandoning them to their own misery. The Hebrew Bible teaches that God exercises "loving kindness, judgment, and righteousness in the earth" (Jeremiah 9:24); the New Testament repeats the idea: "For God so loved the world that he gave his only begotten Son" (John 3:16). Yet, somehow, what we read in the pages of the Bible about God's love doesn't always appear to fit what we see in the pages of our lives, as if we have been reading from the wrong script.

"If I may compare myself to this great teacher and predecessor of ours, Spinoza," wrote former Israeli Supreme Court Justice Haim Cohn, "I would say in his name that the Holocaust is the final and conclusive proof that there can be no God. If there were a God, he would not be a just and merciful God, but a cruel and unjust God, a God of inequity. Not a God who does not slumber and sleep, who watches over his people, or over all mankind, but a God who does not care. Rather than attribute to God cruelty, injustice, and inequity, we, if I may say so, should do him the favor of denying his existence."

Nevertheless, belief in God persists. Millennia of war, pestilence, and famine have eradicated nations, cultures, and families, but amid the rubble and blood, faith re-

15

mains. The Black Death killed an estimated 60 million people in three years, more than the Nazis did in six, yet as the bodies were piled and burned, the families of the corpses traipsed into churches and burned incense to a God whom they worshiped and loved, and whom they believed loved them.

In a Nazi concentration camp in Poland, Jewish children—rounded up from a nearby ghetto—are being slaughtered, their shrieks shattering the air. A Jewish woman, lined up with other prisoners, turns to a German guard and demands a knife. Surprised, the guard hands her a pocketknife. Bending over, she unwraps a bundle of rags. On a snow-white pillow a newborn baby sleeps. She opens the knife and circumcises the child. In a clear, loud voice, she recites the blessing of circumcision: "Blessed art Thou, O Lord our God, King of the Universe, who has sanctified us by thy commandments and has commanded us to perform the circumcision." Then, looking into the sky, she says, "God of the Universe, You have given me a healthy child. I am returning to You a wholesome, kosher Jew." She returns to the German his knife . . . and then hands him her circumcised baby on his snow-white pillow.

Obviously, some people are going to believe in God no matter what. Whether from culture, experience, whatever, some have always been willing to die for their religion. Men and women have been tortured, starved, burned alive because of their religious beliefs, yet they have kept the faith up to their last shriek. How someone could allow himself and his family to be burned alive for a God they have never seen, heard, or touched is a question that they alone could answer. A more pertinent question, though, is: How could this God, in whom they so faithfully believe, allow them to be burned alive to begin with?

In this question is centered man's dilemma with God.

Creation does speak of a loving creator, but the message is Janus-faced: the same halcyon breeze that whispers of God's love can also carry a pestilence that poisons the night with screams. A newborn is a miracle from God, but where is this God and His miracles when the baby is killed, or when he, as an adult, kills?

Many people sense the existence of God. Simple rational thinking says that nothing came from itself. Something had to start this mess. Yet because the world is a mess, questions remain, and the most sensible one, the one that has been asked for millennia, the one that has made more kinetic atheists out of potential saints, is: If a loving Father exists in heaven, why are all His children so unhappy on earth?

The one place that men have searched for the answer, often without finding it, is the biblical book of Job.

17

Two

When Children Die

There is only one truly serious philosophical problem," wrote philosopher Albert Camus, "and that is suicide." "There is only one question which really matters," wrote Rabbi Harold Kushner, "why do bad things happen to good people?"

Two nationalities: one French, one American; two backgrounds: one secular, one religious; two beliefs: God might not exist, God does exist. Despite different presuppositions, approaches, and methods, Camus and Kushner both tasted the fruit on the tree of knowledge of good and evil, partaking mostly of the evil, not to do it themselves, but to understand why it is done. And though picking from the same tree, they had different conclusions about what they ate, what it meant, and why it existed—both wrong!

For Camus, man was doomed to suffer and die, innocent and ultimately alone, amid the "benign silence of the universe." Disease, ignorance, death, and man's inability to know truth from error constituted, for Camus, "the absurd," man's existence in a world where questions, needing answers, had none.

In his novel *The Plague*, Camus portrayed the Algerian town of Oran when swept by pestilence. The plague, a metaphor for war, particularly the Nazi occupation of France (which Camus experienced), symbolized the suffering that has indiscriminately scourged humanity since the beginning of history, the suffering that ultimately made Camus a skeptic.

Within the first month of the pestilence, Jesuit Father Paneloux delivers a sermon to his suddenly overflowing church. While the late arrivals stand outside, and rain drums a monotone drone on their umbrellas, Father Paneloux explains why God smote Oran with *la peste*.

Calamity has come on you, my brethren, and, my brethren, you deserved it. . . . If today the plague is in your midst, that is because the hour has struck for taking thought. The just man need have no fear, but the evildoer has good cause to tremble. For plague is the flail of God and the world His threshing-floor, and implacably He will thresh out His harvest until the wheat is separated from the chaff. . . . You fondly imagined it was enough to visit God on Sundays, and thus you could make free of your weekdays. You believed some brief formalities, some bendings of the knee, would recompense Him well enough for your criminal indifference. But God is not mocked. These brief encounters could not sate the fierce hunger of His love. He wished to see you longer and more often; that is His manner of loving. . . . And this is why, wearied of waiting for you to come to Him, He loosed on you this visitation. . . . And thus, my brothers, at last it is revealed to you, the divine compassion which has ordained good and evil in everything; wrath and pity; the plague and

20

your salvation. This same pestilence which is slaying your works for your good and points your path.

Later, a child, afflicted by the plague, suffers in a hospital bed. Dr. Rieux, symbolizing Camus in his rebellion against Christian theology, and Father Paneloux, symbolizing that theology, helplessly watch as the child, his "flesh wasted to the bone," screams, cries, and convulses. After the child dies, Dr. Rieux confronts Father Paneloux as they leave the hospital. "That child, anyhow, was innocent, and you know it as well as I do!"

When they sit together on a park bench, Father Paneloux responds: "That sort of thing is revolting because it passes our human understanding. But perhaps we should love what we cannot understand."

"No, Father," Rieux says firmly, "I've a very different idea of love. And until my dying day I shall refuse to love the scheme of things in which children are put to torture."

The Jesuit says, "Ah, doctor, I've just realized what is meant by 'grace.' "

In a later sermon, Father Paneloux, in response to that death, says that even though the suffering of a child was humiliating, "since it was God's will, we, too, should will it."

These scenes dramatize the essence of Camus's rebellion against Christianity. Innocent people, even children, unjustly suffer; therefore, if a powerful God rules, leads, and sanctifies this world, then this God is responsible for their suffering. Because Camus understood Christianity to teach that God willed everything, even evil—then for Camus, this God, if He existed, was a murderous tyrant, an unjust and incomprehensible being who brought unpardonable pain upon His creation. To worship this Divine Being, who was the author of evil, was to worship evil itself, something Camus refused to do.

21

Instead, Camus wrote that man lived without hope, without God, and without promise in a world without meaning, an absurd world where all man's cries and prayers ascend no higher than the ceiling.

"I share with you the same horror of evil," Camus told Christians. "But I do not share your hope, and I continue to struggle against this universe where children suffer and die."

In this context, Camus's line about suicide as the only serious philosophical question makes more sense. If life, suffused with pain, disappointment, and injustice, has no meaning, then is life—void of purpose but congested with sorrow—worth living?

"Judging whether or not life is worth living," he wrote, "amounts to answering the fundamental question of philosophy." Though this question seems absurdly pessimistic, people ask it all the time. Every soul contemplating suicide questions whether life is worth the struggle, and many decide it's not. In the Netherlands, where euthanasia is common, about twenty people a day—deciding the pain of living isn't worth it—die at their own request. The issues regarding the "quality of life," abortion, and mercy killing are really modifications of Camus's basic question. He just framed the argument, not in the sphere of medical ethics, but in the broad context of man's general misery, epitomized in that suffering child of Oran.

It was the suffering and death of another child, not one painfully etched on the pages of a novel, but a real one, his own, that prompted Rabbi Kushner on his quest to understand evil. A religious man who had the "image of God as an all-wise, all-powerful parent figure," Rabbi Kushner then learned that his three-year-old son Aaron had a rare disease, progeria, that would cause him to die of "old age" before reaching adolescence. Aaron would "never grow much beyond three feet in height, would have no hair on his head or body, would look like a little old man while he was still a child, and would die in his early teens"—all of which happened. For Rabbi Kushner, the question was: Where was God?

Camus could have answered quickly: a God might be out there, but He's not this "loving Father in heaven" depicted by the Bible, and therefore Aaron was another example of the meaninglessness and absurdity of life. For Rabbi Kushner, however, who believed in God's goodness, that answer wouldn't suffice.

Aaron's death forced Kushner to confront the hard questions for those who believe in a good God. Why do families, even whole communities, unite in fervent prayer for a sick person who dies anyway? If God gives people what they deserve, what did this rabbi do that his son had to suffer and die? And even if the rabbi had done evil, what kind of God would make Aaron, an innocent child, pay? If suffering educates men, what lessons are worth the pain that many go through, often without ever even knowing whatever it was they were supposed to learn to begin with? If the death of a child is to make people more sensitive and caring, then the price, said the rabbi, "is still too high."

Kushner mocked the notion that nothing comes upon us which we cannot bear. "I have seen people crack under the strain of unbearable tragedy. I have seen marriages break up after the death of a child, because parents blamed each other for not taking proper care or for carrying the defective gene, or because the memories they shared were unendurably painful. I have seen some people made noble and sensitive through suffering, but I have seen many more people grow cynical and bitter. . . . If God is testing us, He must know by now that many of us fail the test. If He is only giving us burdens we can bear, I have seen Him miscalculate far too often."

After Aaron's death, the rabbi asked himself, "Can I,

23

in good faith, continue to teach people that the world is good, and that a kind and loving God is responsible for what happens in it?"

He answered no. Unlike Camus, however, who questioned God's existence, Kushner simply revamped his understanding of Him.

God was either all-good, the rabbi concluded, or all-powerful, but not both. Why would an omnipotent God, if He were loving, cause, or even allow, Aaron Kushner to die of progeria? He wouldn't. The only answer, then, is that God was either not as powerful, or as good, as commonly billed.

The rabbi opted for a God who was all-good but not all-powerful. Kushner felt he could worship a God who, though loving man, doesn't have the power to stop evil, rather than worship a God who has the power but, because He is indifferent to man's suffering, doesn't.

Kushner suggests that a randomness exists in creation over which even God Himself has no control. Perhaps God, he speculated, didn't finish creating the earth. This creation process, which replaces chaos with order, still continues. Humans suffer when they become random victims of this lingering chaos. For example, God doesn't will that an earthquake kill 60,000 people in Armenia. Nor does God allow the earthquake to happen. Actually, God has no power to stop it. It just happens, without purpose, meaning, or conscience because there are parts of the earth where God does not yet have sovereignty. Tragedies "happen at random, and randomness is another name for chaos, in those corners of the universe where God's creative light has not yet penetrated. And chaos is evil; not wrong, not malevolent, but evil nonetheless, because by causing tragedies at random, it prevents people from believing in God's goodness."

According to Kushner, God does not abandon us as the

unfortunate victims of chance. Maybe God can't stop these calamities, but He can comfort us when they happen. Kushner's God is a God of compassion, not power, a God of understanding, not providence. God might not have anything to do with our trials. He might not be able to stop them. Perhaps stopping tragedy is not even His job. Nevertheless, He will help us through them once they occur.

For Kushner, our question shouldn't be, Why did God bring this tragedy, or even allow it to happen? Instead, we should say, OK, God, what happens now that tragedy has struck?

Camus and Kushner, a philosopher and a rabbi, a skeptic and a Jew, put into their own words the basic sorrow of all our souls. Camus's line about suicide being the only serious philosophical question, Kushner's about why bad things happen to good people—were simply two different approaches to the same timeless dilemma of suffering. Both men tasted its fruit, and though agreeing only that it was bitter, their conclusions about what caused it, and why, were wrong.

Camus's God, as portrayed in *The Plague*, grossly perverts the God depicted in the Bible. If God were as portrayed by Father Paneloux, then Camus had reason to rebel. Camus remained justifiably skeptical about a God who, trying to "sate the fierce hunger of His love," smites a town with a pestilence that painfully obliterates thousands, all just to get the survivors into church more.

Through the suffering child, Camus spat upon Father Paneloux's assertion that "the just man need have no fear" because only the evil will suffer, a teaching that has no more basis in either Christian theology, or reality, than does Rudolph the Red-Nosed Reindeer. The Jesuit's statements that they should, perhaps, love the suffering of a child, and that because "it was God's will, we, too, should will it"—gnarls the truth about the character of

God. Camus, apparently, never understood the Bible teaching about evil, and considering the nonsense on the topic spewed out over the centuries by Christians (symbolized by Paneloux), it's no wonder he didn't.

Kushner, with Judaism as his base for attempting to analyze evil, comes much closer to truth than did Camus, who didn't have Kushner's presuppositions about a loving God. Kushner knew enough to know that, despite suffering and evil, a good God existed. Unlike Camus, he knew that God didn't bring evil upon humanity, that it came from somewhere else. He just didn't understand from where.

His assertion that "suppose that Creation, the process of replacing chaos with order, were still going on" contradicts the teaching of his own Hebrew Bible, which reads that "the heavens and the earth were finished, and all the host of them" (Genesis 2:1). The word for "finished" comes from the Hebrew word which means just that: *complete, finished.* Nothing in the Bible teaches that God is still creating the earth. That concept is alien to fundamental Jewish or Christian theology.

His first false assumption, that God hasn't finished the creation process, led him to a bigger one: that God is not able to control the randomness that supposedly exists where His "creative light has not yet penetrated." While Camus sees an evil God, Kushner sees a diminished one.

Kushner's God, though He made the earth, can't control the events on it, like a child who rolls a fist-size snowball down a hill until it becomes so big he loses control and it smashes through a fence. The child who created the snowball couldn't keep it from destroying the fence. The best he can do is, after the fact, mend the damage.

Rabbi Kushner comes up with such a wishy-washy God because he takes a wishy-washy view of the Bible. Unlike Camus, Kushner believed he could find answers in the

26

Bible, yet he so allegorized, poeticized, and spiritualized the Scripture that he neutralized the answers he sought within its pages.

Like everyone who writes about suffering in the context of the Bible, Kushner used the biblical book of Job. He devoted an entire chapter to Job because it does help explain "why bad things happen to good people." Yet the reason that commentators like Kushner rarely find satisfactory answers in Job is that they don't read the book for what it says. Instead, they make Job into an allegory, a parable, a poeticized fantasy or fiction—interpretations akin to analyzing a Renoir by studying only a black-and-white print.

Instead, the only way to understand how evil and suffering can exist in a universe created by a loving God is to take the book of Job literally. Job must be taken literally, or not at all—because literally is the only way it works! Job, literally, goes behind the scenes of things unseen, to the root of all sorrow. Job, not allegorized or spiritualized, gives a relatively complete, full-color picture of how a loving God can exist in heaven while we're such wretches here on earth. Any other approach gives only what Rabbi Kushner got: vague shades of gray.

Job, adulterated or diluted, gives only adulterated or diluted answers. For those, however, who know better than Camus's existential emptiness, or Kushner's denuded deity, answers abound in the book of Job, literally.

Three

Funhouse Mirror

In his highly acclaimed play *J.B.*, poet Archibald MacLeish created a wealthy, successful family man who praised God for his prosperity.

"Not for a watch-tick," says J.B., snug inside his New England home, "have I doubted / God was on my side, was good to me. / Even young and poor knew it. / People call it luck: it wasn't. / I never thought so from the first / fine silver dollar to the last / controlling interest in some company / I couldn't get—and got. It isn't / luck."

Sarah, too, J.B.'s suburban wife, knowing of divine goodness, explains to the children over a steaming Thanksgiving turkey, "God doesn't give all this for nothing: / a good home, good food, / father, mother, brothers, sisters. / We too have our part to play. / If we do our part He does His, / He always has."

But then two drunk soldiers stumble into the house with the news that J.B. and Sarah's son had been killed after the war in which he fought had already ended. Next a son and daughter are smeared across the road by a

29

drunk driver in a head-on collision. A second daughter is raped, murdered, and dumped near a lumberyard. Finally an earthquake destroys all their financial assets, leaving them in economic ruin.

Her finely woven theology crushed like spiderweb under a boot, Sarah hisses: "God is our enemy."

J.B. takes a different view. "God is there too, in the desperation. / I do not know why God should strike / but God is what is stricken also: . . . The Lord / giveth . . . Say it. . . . the Lord taketh away. . . ."

"Takes!" Sarah screams, "Kills! Kills! Kills! Kills!"

In his novel *The Undying Fire,* H. G. Wells penned the despair of the European humanists whose hope that the twentieth century would usher in an age of peace and prosperity vanished amid the trenches and gas of the First World War. The main character, Job Huss, complains: "Suddenly, swiftly, I have had misfortune following upon misfortune—without cause or justification. I am thrown into the darkest doubt and dismay. The universe seems harsh and black to me; whereas formerly I believed that at the core of it and universally pervading it was the Will of a God of light. Men and women have died in that illusion of security. But this war has torn away the veil of illusion from millions of men. . . . Mankind is coming of age. We can see life at last for what it is and what it is not."

One a play, one a novel, *J.B.* and *The Undying Fire* both rested on a common base: they portrayed the ancient epic of Job in modern terms. Each struggled with the lost hope that despite the carnage of human existence, goodness and righteousness would prevail, and that behind all the injustice and indignity of life a good and noble purpose would ultimately triumph. For the characters in *J.B.* and *The Undying Fire*, that hope is battered, even crushed. With pessimism, disillusionment, and doubt as much a part of life as is breath, it's no wonder that millennia after the epic was scribbled on a scroll in some ancient Near Eastern desert, the story of Job—brooding with pessimism, disillusionment, and doubt—is still studied, analyzed, and (as MacLeish, Wells, and others have shown) mimicked.

Unlike its modern imitations, however, which occur in a definite time and place, the book of Job remains as elusive as a shadow in regard to who wrote it, where, even when. While many other biblical books, whose basic setting, time frame, even authors can be determined, Job basks in ambiguity. The disputed dates of its creation—anywhere from 1500 B.C. (the time of Moses) to 300 B.C. (the time of Persian King Ahasuerus)—are about as precise as knowing only that a date fell somewhere between the early centuries of Islam to the Ayatollah's overthrow of the Shah of Iran. Jewish tradition holds that Moses wrote Job; others contend that editors hacked and pecked on the script for centuries. And while most of the other biblical books deal with Jews and Israelite history, Job remains distinctly outside that tradition, set only in an ancient Near Eastern land that still can't be located on a map. Hovering in history, not rooted to specifics, Job raises questions about suffering in the context of general humanity, rather than in the milieu of one distinct nation and people.

"The whole earth," says a character in *The Undying Fire*, "is now—Job."

He's right. To understand Job, his suffering, and the causes behind it, is to understand that Job is a reflection, however exaggerated, of all humanity. We all, each in our own way, are like Job. All, like Job, have rejoiced in triumph—and all, like Job, have languished in despair. And many, misunderstanding the cause of their anguish, have, like Job, blamed God for the pain. The only difference: Job's experiences, his heights and depths, joys and sorrows, faith and doubts, were just more extreme than ours.

31

Indeed, Job's heights were so high that even God declared that "there is none like him in the earth, a perfect and an upright man, one that feareth God, and escheweth evil" (Job 1:8). For God—who, in another place in the Bible, says of men, "There is none that doeth good, no, not one" (Psalm 14:3)—to call Job perfect and upright means that Job must have been something!

He was. First, he had accumulated great wealth: "seven thousand sheep, and three thousand camels, and five hundred yoke of oxen, and five hundred she asses" (Job 1:3), big bucks back then. And though material greatness does not necessarily reveal righteousness (if so, Donald Trump, Leona Helmsley, and Michael Milken would sprout wings), Job used his money to help the poor and suffering (see Job 31), actions that revealed the goodness within him.

Job sired seven sons and three daughters, a close-knit family as well. In many societies of the ancient Near East, where women were regarded as property, and often bartered like cattle—Job's sons invited their sisters to a feast, not to wait on or clean tables, but to party with the boys instead. "And his sons went and feasted in their houses, every one his day; and sent and called for their three sisters to eat and to drink with them" (Job 1:4). Apparently, Job's family reflected the kindness, generosity, and love that exuded from his own life.

A devout follower of the Lord, Job continually "rose up early in the morning, and offered burnt offerings" (Job 1:5) in behalf of his children, whom he feared might have sinned against God. Job apparently understood something about the Ten Commandments too (see Job 31) because he knew that cursing God—even in the heart— was wrong (the third commandment); he didn't commit adultery (the seventh commandment); he didn't covet things that weren't his (the tenth commandment); he didn't lie and deceive (the eighth commandment); and he had no other gods before the Lord (the first commandment). Job's life fulfilled the words given to ancient Israel, and then repeated by Jesus thousands of years later: " 'You shall love the Lord your God with all your heart, with all your soul, and with all your mind,' " and " 'you shall love your neighbor as yourself' " (Matthew 22:37, 39, NKJV).

Devout, generous, selfless, Job had a large loving family whom he himself loved. With all the wealth, family, and prosperity he enjoyed, as well as the love, patience, and kindness he exhibited, no wonder the Bible says that "this man was the greatest of all the men of the east" (Job 1:3).

Of course, few have enjoyed Job's prosperity, either spiritual or material. Nevertheless, Job reflects all humanity, even if the image, like in a funhouse mirror, is exaggerated and extreme. Who has not, if only for a span as fleeting as a dream, enjoyed some happiness and fulfillment? Whether a derelict, who has known only dirty alleys, slipping for one night between dry sheets, his grumbling stomach now calmed with warm food; or a teenager, flunking school, exulting over a passed exam where the only red mark on the paper is the A at the top of the page—all have enjoyed at least a flicker of contentment, a spark of optimism. Who, if just for a moment, has not experienced the joy of love, or of being loved? What man or woman, sifting through even the darkest images of their past, could not find even a flicker of light, a moment of happiness? Job, in his light and glory, as bright as it was, is us, in our light and glory, as dim as it might be in comparison.

Yet, as Job learned, no matter how bright the light, or glorious the shine, it can be quickly snuffed, and darkness will fill the void.

On a day when all the children were eating and drinking wine in the house of Job's eldest son, a messenger

33

runs to Job with the words: "The oxen were plowing, and the asses feeding beside them: And the Sabeans fell upon them, and took them away; yea, they have slain the servants with the edge of the sword; and I only am escaped alone to tell thee" (Job 1:14, 15).

Another messenger follows with more bad news: "The fire of God is fallen from heaven, and hath burned up the sheep, and the servants, and consumed them; and I only am escaped alone to tell thee" (Job 1:16).

Then, a third messenger says: "The Chaldeans made out three bands, and fell upon the camels, and have carried them away, yea, and slain the servants with the edge of the sword; and I only am escaped alone to tell thee" (Job 1:17).

Next, a final messenger appears with news of the greatest tragedy that could befall a parent: "Thy sons and daughters were eating and drinking wine in their eldest brother's house: And, behold, there came a great wind from the wilderness, and smote the four corners of the house, and it fell upon the young men, and they are dead; and I only am escaped alone to tell thee" (Job 1:18, 19).

Despite a lifetime of prosperity and happiness, in just a few moments, all that Job had and loved he lost. Who could grasp the sadness, confusion, and panic that must have overwhelmed him? Then, when Job probably thought the tragedies ended, his skin, from "the soul of his foot unto his crown" (Job 2:7), erupted with fierce boils. Job—who had been recognized not only as the "greatest man of the east," but, according to God, even in all the earth (Job 1:8)—became a blubbering, sobbing, and wailing wreck reduced to rags as he sat amid ashes and mourned.

Here, too, Job grotesquely reflects ourselves, no matter how exaggerated. We don't need to have our fortune, children, and health wiped out in order to know the despair, heartache, and misery that caused Job to exclaim: "Oh, that my grief were thoroughly weighed, and my calamity laid in the balances together! For now it would be heavier than the sand of the sea" (Job 6:2, 3). Who hasn't had moments, days, even months, when Job's cry—"I should have been carried from the womb to the grave!" (Job 10:19)—was theirs? Who, when disaster struck, hasn't been tempted, like Job, to blame God: "For the arrows of the Almighty are within me, the poison whereof drinketh up my spirit: the terrors of God do set themselves in array against me" (Job 6:2, 3)? Which of us—framed in bone, cushioned by flesh, and covered with skin—hasn't experienced how fragile and untrustworthy the whole package can be! "My flesh is clothed with worms and clods of dust," Job cried, "my skin is broken, and become loathsome. My days are swifter than a weaver's shuttle, and are spent without hope" (Job 7:5, 6).

These tragedies all occurred in the beginning of the story. From the first raid by the Sabeans until the last boil to erupt on Job's skin, everything took place in the first two chapters in the epic, which is forty-two chapters long. The rest of the chapters deal with conversations between Job and three friends—Eliphaz, Bildad, Zophar—and later a fourth, Elihu, who visit Job in his affliction and give eloquent speeches regarding God, suffering, and justice. Finally, God Himself appears "out of the whirlwind" (Job 38:1), confronts them all, and eventually restores to Job more than he had before the calamities struck: "And the Lord turned the captivity of Job, when he prayed for his friends: also the Lord gave Job twice as much as he had before. . . . So the Lord blessed the latter end of Job more than his beginning: for he had fourteen thousand sheep, and six thousand camels, and a thousand yoke of oxen, and a thousand she asses. He had also seven sons and three daughters. . . . After this lived Job an hundred and forty years, and saw his sons, and his sons' sons, even four generations" (Job 42:10-16).

Though life turned around for Job at the end, the bulk of the story took place during Job's affliction, when he conversed with his friends, and even God. These talks contain some of the most sublime poetry ever penned, and they are the focus of most study and commentary on the book.

Yet the speeches, though eloquent, don't explain why "bad things happen to good people." They consist mainly of the words of Job who, claiming his innocence, laments his suffering while his friends, seeking to understand what has happened, accuse him of wrongdoing.

"Remember," says Eliphaz the Temanite, "I pray thee, who ever perished, being innocent? or where were the righteous cut off? Even as I have seen, they that plow iniquity, and sow wickedness, reap the same" (Job 4:7, 8).

But Job knows that, whatever the cause of his misery, he has done nothing to deserve it—just as Rabbi Kushner knew that he did nothing to bring progeria to his son Aaron, just as Rieux knew that the dying child didn't deserve the plague. "My face is foul with weeping," Job cries, "and on my eyelids is the shadow of death; not for any injustice in mine hands: also my prayer is pure. O earth, cover not thou my blood, and let my cry have no place. Also now, behold, my witness is in heaven, and my record is on high" (Job 16:16-19).

Even God, in His speeches at the end of the book, doesn't explain why humans suffer. Instead, He confronts Job with His own majesty and power in His creation, in contrast to Job's weakness and lack of knowledge: "Where wast thou when I laid the foundations of the earth?" God questions Job. "Declare, if thou hast understanding. Who hath laid the measures thereof, if thou knowest? or who hath stretched the line upon it? Whereupon are the foundations thereof fastened? or who laid the corner stone thereof?" "Hast thou commanded the morning since thy days; and caused the dayspring to know his place? . . . Hast thou entered into the springs of the sea? or hast thou walked in the search of the depth?" (Job 38:4-6, 12-16).

The conversations between Job and his friends, even between Job and God, and the subsequent turn in Job's fortunes, don't reveal the cause of suffering. If anything, most of what Job's friends say about injustice and trials is wrong, and God chastises them for it: "My wrath is kindled against thee," God says to Eliphaz, "and against thy two friends, for ye have not spoken of me the thing that is right" (Job 42:7).

Answers to these question, however, do exist in the book, and they are found within the first two chapters, before the speeches begin. And here, the key is not what happens in the natural, visible world, but in the supernatural, invisible world behind it.

Imagine standing alone in an empty room with only a radio. The radio is off, the room silent. Nothing, nobody is there, except what you see, which is the radio, and what you hear, which is nothing. You then turn on the radio and run the dial across the stations. Music, laughter, news, advertisement blurs across your ears. Suddenly the room, which moments before was silent, now bursts with noise. But from where? Was the sound packed in the radio itself, only to be released when you freed it? Of course not. The sound, in another form, was in the room the whole time. Yet you had no idea. Why? Because you weren't tuned in! Your senses, no matter how acute, can't pick up radio waves even though they exist all around you!

The supernatural operates on the same principle. Unaided, we can be no more aware of the existence of the supernatural activity around us any more than, without a receiver, we can be aware of the frequencies that surround us too. Like radio waves, the supernatural is everywhere—but, in our natural state, we are tuned out. Job tunes us in.

A person—exposed to intense radiation for weeks— hears, smells, sees, feels, senses, and tastes none of it. He has no idea that billions of radioactive particles are bombarding his body—until the results: vomiting, hair loss, disease, death.

The same with the supernatural. We see, feel, and suffer the results, but cannot discern the real cause. We can't. It is hidden, concealed behind a veil.

Job, the first two chapters, lifts that veil.

CHAPTER

Four

Star Wars

How ironic that fortunes have been spent in this century, filming, producing, and watching science fiction flicks—when the real space drama rages around us. Mr. Spock, Darth Vader, or E.T. are household names, yet few know the characters involved in the true battle, the ultimate in star wars. Mesmerized by the adventures of Luke Skywalker or Captain Kirk, millions of people know nothing of a cosmic conflict that has been waging for millennia—a conflict that will soon climax here on earth. About fifty years ago Orson Welles read *War of the Worlds* over the airwaves and panicked thousands who feared that Martians had invaded New Jersey—yet few today comprehend the real invasion of earth.

That is, unless they believe the book of Job.

The story starts with the patriarch, surrounded by an Eden-like aura, enjoying great material prosperity along with a large, loving family. As far as Job and his family are concerned, peace exists on earth; in another part of the universe, however, a battle rages.

> Now there was a day when the sons of God came
> to present themselves before the Lord, and Satan
> came also among them. And the Lord said unto
> Satan, Whence comest thou? Then Satan answered
> the Lord, and said, From going to and fro in the
> earth, and from walking up and down in it. And the
> Lord said unto Satan, Hast thou considered my ser-
> vant Job, that there is none like him in the earth, a
> perfect and an upright man, one that feareth God,
> and escheweth evil? Then Satan answered the Lord,
> and said, Doth Job fear God for nought? Hast not
> thou made an hedge about him, and about his house,
> and about all that he hath on every side? Thou hast
> blessed the work of his hands, and his substance is
> increased in the land. But put forth thine hand now,
> and touch all that he hath, and he will curse thee to
> thy face. And the Lord said unto Satan, Behold, all
> that he hath is in thy power; only upon himself put
> not forth thine hand. So Satan went forth from the
> presence of the Lord (Job 1:6-12).

Next, Satan, this space invader, comes to earth and ruins the patriarch financially. He then kills Job's ten children. When Job stays faithful to God anyway, the story shifts back to the cosmic setting, where Satan again challenges God concerning Job: "Skin for skin, yea, all that a man hath will he give for his life. Put forth thine hand now, and touch his bone and his flesh, and he will curse thee to thy face. And the Lord said unto Satan, Behold, he is in thine hand, but save his life" (Job 2:4-6). Still hidden, this evil extraterrestrial returns to earth and smites Job with boils.

These initial scenes, so crucial to understanding Job, are usually spiritualized and allegorized into nothing but metaphors of good and evil concocted by superstitious ancients who, unaware of natural law and science, sought supernatural explanations for natural events. But, unless this section is taken literally, Job becomes nothing but allegory, akin to trying to understand the formation of American democracy while believing that James Madison and Thomas Jefferson were made-up figures used to symbolize the nation's early days. Starting with that false presupposition about Jefferson and Madison, a person would arrive at false conclusions regarding the origin of American democracy! The same principle works with Job. Start out with the false assumption that these early chapters are mere allegory, and you will arrive—like Rabbi Kushner and others—at false conclusions about suffering.

Because the modern mind has been programmed to equate extraterrestrials with science fiction, many find it hard to believe that real ones exist. Yet unmistakably revealed in the billions of galaxies spinning across the cosmos, in the single atom, and everything in between, is the existence of God—the supreme "extraterrestrial."

Of course, the existence of God doesn't necessarily prove the reality of other nonearthly life too. Yet with all the galaxies in the known universe, each shimmering like an infinity of flaming crystal, it's the epitome of ethnocentricity to believe that we, on this little planet, a faint spark amid blazes of celestial glory, are alone.

"I feel nearly certain that [this] galaxy will turn out to be rich with life, of many shapes and sizes, and that any civilization we contact will be far wiser than we," said Harvard physicist Paul Horowitz, who—with a radio telescope that monitors 8.4 million space radio channels simultaneously—has for years been scanning the universe in search of extraterrestrials. Since the 1960s, scientists like Horowitz have been involved in dozens of efforts to find extraterrestrial life. Awed by the dimensions of the universe, many astronomers and physicists are certain, by sheer odds alone, that life must exist elsewhere. Frank Drake, Dean of Natural Science at the University of California, estimated that at least 10,000 extraterrestrial civilizations must exist in the Milky Way, which is just one galaxy. Current instruments detect about 10 billion other galaxies, many larger than our own. Beyond them spin probably billions and billions of others, each containing an endless number of suns, each sun possibly the center of a solar system like ours. Even if only one inhabited planet existed *per galaxy* (instead of Drake's 10,000), billions of other civilizations would populate the universe. Numbers like these have convinced scientists involved in the search for extraterrestrial intelligence that we are not alone.

We're not. As the book of Job has so graphically revealed, other extraterrestrial life exists. But while scientists like Paul Horowitz scan the stars year after year, their ears attuned to expensive equipment in hopes of hearing even a peep, twitter, or mutter from some alien being, all in order to know just *if* other life even exists— Job not only reveals that it does, but gives insight into its nature.

First, it reveals a powerful extraterrestrial, one hostile, not only to God but to man. This alien, called in the Bible Satan (which means Adversary), had invaded the earth. Twice when asked where he came from, he replied: "From going to and fro in the earth, and from walking up and down in it" (Job 1:7; 2:2). Though stalking across the planet, he appears also in another part of the universe as well, where God Himself dwells. Apparently, unbounded by the restraints of time and space, he is able to travel across the cosmos. Even Darth Vader needed a spaceship. This extraterrestrial, apparently, doesn't.

Also, the Bible shows that this being was an intelligent student of humanity, probably because he spent time here. He understood human nature, which is why he taunted God, saying that Job served Him, not out of any selfless motives ("Does Job fear God for naught?"), but only out of self-interest. This extraterrestrial knew man's selfishness, greed, and desire for gain. He implied that Job served God only because God had blessed him, but if life soured for Job, God would then see what His "faithful servant" was really made of. Understanding man's desire for self-preservation, the Adversary was certain that if Job were physically harmed, he would curse God.

"Skin for skin," Satan said to God, "yea, all that a man hath will he give for his life. But put forth thine hand now, and touch his bone and his flesh, and he will curse thee to thy face" (Job 2:4, 5). Here, too, the Adversary appears to be an astute observer of human nature in general, (if not of Job in particular).

Also, by inciting the Sabeans and the Chaldeans to attack Job's property, this extraterrestrial revealed the ability to influence men's minds, causing them even to steal and kill. He apparently controlled Job's wife, who, by telling Job to "curse God and die," was unknowingly trying to make Job do exactly what the Adversary wanted him to. He possesses supernatural strength also, for he dropped out of the sky a fire mighty enough to devour Job's sheep and servants. Because the Adversary was able to bring a fierce wind, perhaps a tornado, that blew down the house of Job's eldest son and killed the children, the book reveals that he manifests some control over nature as well. Finally, his smiting Job with boils shows that he has power to afflict humanity with disease. Obviously, not only intelligent, this extraterrestrial is potent beyond comprehension.

And nasty too. Destroying all of Job's possessions, killing his children, afflicting the old man with disease, even using Job's wife against her husband, all just to try to reveal what he believed were Job's selfish motives, this space alien has revealed himself as so pernicious that he makes fictional demons like Darth Vader look no more threatening than the Good Tooth Fairy.

His most dangerous aspect, however, is elusiveness. Like radio waves, he is everywhere, but unseen, unsensed, unnoticed. Who's going to fear, or even fight, an enemy so concealed that most people snicker at the idea of his existence? What foe could be more dangerous than one who, after he attacks, makes his victim think that someone else, even God, did the attacking while he, the real nemesis, walks away undetected?

"The fire of God," the messenger said, "is fallen from heaven" (Job 1:16), even though the Adversary dropped the flames. Job's friends said that God brought these calamities upon Job. Job himself blamed God. This extraterrestrial's greatest weapon is, clearly, not only his ability to hide himself, but to make God look like the one doing all the dirty work!

By exposing the Adversary, however, the Bible deprives this invader of his sneakiest ploy. Like a radio snatching waves out of the air and converting them into sound, the book of Job reveals not only the existence of this hostile creature, but his tactics and character as well. By lifting the veil between the seen and the unseen, the Bible warns us about a cosmic being able to transcend the barriers of time and space, a being so deceptive in his evil that he makes his victims blame God for the suffering that he himself causes.

This aspect, the one of blame, is a crucial truth in Job. Though everyone blamed God for the calamities (just as Sarah did in *J.B.* and Father Paneloux in *The Plague*), the real culprit was this alien. If anything, the book of Job shows God as the source of all good. Even the Adversary says to the Lord concerning Job, "Hast not thou made an hedge about him, and about his house, and about all that he hath on every side? thou hast blessed the work of his

44

hands, and his substance is increased in the land" (Job 1:10). The enemy himself admits that God has given Job all his blessing. Not until this nasty extraterrestrial appeared did death, suffering, and tears appear as well.

Job, in a sense, repeats the Garden of Eden epic. No matter if one takes the story literally or allegorically, everything in Eden was blissful until the intruder appeared. Once he did, sorrow followed.

In that account, God first created the earth. "And God saw every thing that he had made, and behold, it was very good" (Genesis 1:31). He then created man and put him in a garden: "And the Lord God planted a garden eastward in Eden; and there he put the man whom he had formed" (Genesis 2:8). There, with "every tree that is pleasant to the sight, and good for food" (verse 9), Adam lived with his wife, where they were to "be fruitful and multiply" (Genesis 1:28). Job's situation, great material blessings, and a large family, reflected this prototypical Edenic scene.

When the intruder appeared, however, this time in the guise of a serpent (see Genesis 3:1, Revelation 12:9), he led Adam and Eve into sin by tempting them to disobey a clear command of God. As a result of his intrusion, pain and suffering followed. Both the Edenic and Jobian accounts reveal the true cause of happiness (God), and suffering (the Adversary).

After Adam fell, he blamed God by saying, "The woman whom *thou* gavest to be with me, she gave me of the tree, and I did eat" (Genesis 3:12). Thousands of years have passed, and God is still being blamed for men's suffering, just as He was in Eden, in Job, in *J.B.*, and in *The Undying Fire*, just as He is now.

Though Job's accusers believed that God, for whatever reason, brought these calamities upon him, God was not the cause of Job's troubles any more than He was of Adam's in the Eden epic. To attribute evil to God is to attribute it to a supernatural force, but the wrong one!

45

People, ready to blame God for disaster, snicker at the idea of Satan, even though he is the primary, if not always the direct cause, of all suffering on earth.

It is this cosmic intruder, not God, who incites men to steal, to murder, plunder, and pillage. The Adversary, not God, initiates the disease, the suffering, and the disasters that batter the earth black and blue. The Adversary defaces the earth, only he vandalizes it so craftily and artfully that those looking at the original piece think that the defects are part of the original creation! Yet suffering was no more God's original intent for man than the explosion on the *Challenger* was NASA's plan for the space shuttle.

A cool sea breeze, a grove bright with oranges, a mother breast-feeding her infant, all testify to the love and character of the Creator. But a typhoon washing away villages, a blight that extinguishes the orange glow, a mother strangling her infant, all testify to an intruder, an unwanted invader defacing the creation and eradicating the image of God from man. Evil and good are not philosophy, semantics, and poetry, but literal realities embodied in supernatural entities contending for the souls of men.

Like nuclear fission, the enemy ignited the first few sparks, and everything else followed in an endless explosion of sin, suffering, and death. God gave men marriage and sex, and men, under supernatural influence, become adulterers and pornographers. God stocked the earth with material blessings, yet greedy, selfish, and inconsiderate men horde it and so others live without shelter, food, or clothing. God gave us the gift of speech, and men lie, curse, and insult. On and on it goes, an endless chain reaction of pain, violence, and sin that has been multiplying and incessantly feeding itself since the enemy first made inroads on this planet. He simply lurks behind the shadows, constantly blowing on cinders in order to keep everything as hot as possible.

Of course, a woman who smokes for fifty years and is dying of cancer can't blame Satan for giving her the disease. He didn't have to. He simply enticed her to smoke. The cigarettes did the rest. Like a traitor who opens a city gate at night to allow enemy soldiers in, and then is killed by those same soldiers, humans are often this extraterrestrial's most effective agents for their own pain and destruction, or (as the bands of Sabeans and Chaldeans showed) for the pain and destruction of others.

Like Job, however, most people have no idea what is happening to them, why, or what is causing it. "The devil," comedian Flip Wilson jested, "made me do it." He probably did, though who believes it? Suffering is usually attributed to chance, to the inevitable tragedies of life, or to God. As the book of Job shows, neither answer is correct.

But accepting the idea of Satan, of this supernatural bogeyman who has invaded the earth for the purpose of wreaking havoc on us poor earthlings, leaves us with a number of questions. Perhaps the first, and most obvious, is: Where is God?

If God is so powerful that He can create and sustain billions of galaxies, if He is so full of compassion that, as the Bible says, "His mercy endureth for ever"—why hasn't He zapped the intruder? Why has He allowed this extraterrestrial to afflict men with disease, or inspire them to murder, steal, and lie? If the Adversary can bring a famine to Ethiopia, why hasn't the Lord, "who made heaven and earth, the sea, and all that in them is," bring rain before the first innocent child dried up like a raisin and died? If Satan inspired Treblinka, why didn't God blot out the camp before it killed the first Jew? What kind of God, who has the power to end evil but doesn't, asks people to love Him "with all thine heart, with all thy soul, and with all thy might"?

Here, too, Job—in those first two chapters—has answers.

CHAPTER
Five

A Question of Character

So far, the book of Job has revealed two "extra-terrestrials": God and the Adversary. Yet other nonearthly intelligent life exists as well. Both times, when the story shifts from the earthly to the heavenly, these aliens appear.

"Now there was a day when the *sons of God* came to present themselves before the Lord, and Satan came also among them" (Job 1:6, emphasis supplied). The next chapter starts: "Again there was a day when the *sons of God* came to present themselves before the Lord, and Satan came also among them" (Job 2:1, emphasis supplied).

Each time the reader is told of these "sons of God." The author, somehow privy to these cosmic councils, describes these beings presenting themselves before God. Nothing else is said about them. Nothing else needs to be. Their existence alone is what counts.

Whatever their purpose, they do not appear directly involved in the conflict. The most that can be deduced is

49

that they hover on the sidelines, watching. Yet that point alone, the one of their watching, is the crucial reason why God had not immediately eradicated the Adversary.

Close to the conflict, but not taking part, these "sons of God" witness the turmoil between God and Satan, a battle not over land, territory, or material possessions, but over loyalty, love, and faithfulness. The Adversary claims that Job served God out of selfishness only, and that once adversity struck, Job would be no more loyal than a fat tabby who sniffs out a meal down the street.

Though at first glance, Job seems to be the one on trial—God really is. By impugning Job's motives for being faithful, the Adversary attacks God Himself. If God was so good, so wonderful, then Job would worship Him out of love and appreciation alone. Instead, by asserting that Job served Him out of personal selfishness, the Adversary implies that perhaps God isn't so good, forgiving, and loving after all. If so, Job would serve Him no matter what. By claiming that Job would turn against Him once things went wrong, the Adversary, however subtly, insinuates that even Job himself has questions about God.

This conflict concerning God's character is not a private dispute. The Adversary accuses God before these other cosmic entities. They, better than any of the humans in the story (who know nothing about the celestial skirmishes), can clearly see the issues. These intelligences, specifically mentioned as present when Satan accused the Lord, apparently have a interest in what happens between God and this evil extraterrestrial. Perhaps they have questions about the character of God themselves?

For these reasons, then, God did not simply destroy the Adversary. He could have declared: "How dare you question Me?" and then done to the Adversary what the Adversary did to Job's children. Yet God's character is being questioned in front of these other extraterrestrials.

Had He simply eradicated His enemy at the first sign of insubordination, then the accusations about His goodness and mercy could have appeared well founded!

Throughout the Bible, from Genesis to Revelation, God is described as merciful, just, patient, kind, forgiving, fair, compassionate, and loving. "But thou, O Lord, art a God merciful and gracious, slow to anger and abounding in steadfast love and faithfulness" (Psalm 86:15, RSV). "Justice and judgment are the habitation of thy throne: mercy and truth shall go before thy face" (Psalm 89:14). "The Lord God, merciful, and gracious, longsuffering, and abundant in goodness and truth" (Exodus 34:6). If, at the first sign of trouble, God had simply wasted—destroyed—His accuser, He would have appeared no more just, fair, or compassionate than a fascist who—at the first inkling of insubordination— mercilessly, without compassion or justice, eliminates his enemies. It's that particular aspect of a fascist, the absolute, unquestionable, and relentless use of the iron rod against any opposition that makes the fascist what he is.

But God is no fascist. He is a benevolent King who runs the universe by moral laws—and, without violating these laws, He will end the problem of evil in a just and open manner before these other onlooking intelligences.

As Creator, God certainly had the prerogative to immediately eradicate the Adversary, or any other insubordinate in His creation. Yet it would have been contradictory for a Power who constantly pictures Himself as merciful, patient, and compassionate to wipe out opposition the moment it arises. Nothing about that eradication would fit the attributes that God has consistently used throughout the Bible to describe Himself.

Instead, not only would arbitrary violence have been out of character, it could have made the Adversary's accusations against God seem right. Those celestials watching the battle, if they hadn't had questions about

51

God's character before He eradicated the accuser, certainly might have had some after. They might have even begun serving God out of selfish interest, such as fear of being blotted out themselves!

God, therefore, chose not to instantly obliterate the enemy. Instead, He took a different approach—one harmonious with His own character of love, patience, and justice.

The essential element, then, is those "sons of God." They reveal that we are not alone. Other life exists in the universe, and, as the book of Job shows, it is interested in the conflict between God and the Adversary. God will deal with this evil extraterrestrial in a manner not only open before other intelligences, but in sync with the attributes of His character.

The central question in these two chapters (indeed the whole story) doesn't deal with the character of Job, as to whether or not he will remain faithful. As important as that aspect is, it is nevertheless secondary. Rather, the real question deals with the character of God Himself: What is He like? Is He as good as He bills Himself? Why does He allow evil to continue? Should He be worshiped for any reasons other than His own goodness?

For devout Christians, Jews, or anyone who believes in a loving Creator, the dilemma of suffering is really a dilemma about God. What kind of God allows earthquakes to crush, wars to maim, and diseases to kill? Questions about suffering ask more about God than about pain. The book of Job, more than confronting the issue of why men suffer, confronts the issue of the character of God, which is often questioned, even defamed, in the framework of human agony. For this reason, then, the questions in Job about the character of God are confronted in the context of suffering, because it is always in this context, the one of suffering, that they are asked.

The conflict between God an His enemy obviously involves man, or why else would God, in challenging the Adversary, point to a man (in this case, Job) unless man were not somehow involved? The battle also deals with character, fidelity, and faithfulness, or why else would God have raised the question of Job's strengths in these areas, and why would the Adversary go to extraordinary lengths to try and undermine them? Man's character, then, must be a crucial factor in this controversy between God and Satan.

The dialogue between God and this evil extraterrestrial makes it easy to extrapolate on the nature of the battle. The Adversary wandered the earth, making men as miserable and wretched as he could (Job, a prime example). Then, depending upon their response, he would taunt God with the results, all before these onlooking "sons of God." Satan, apparently, is fighting the battle against God by wreaking havoc on man and trying to turn him against his Creator. For whatever reason, God has chosen to link Himself, and the vindication of His name, with us. Because the real issue is the character of God, the Adversary therefore tried to undermine God by undermining man.

God first brought man, specifically Job, into the picture, by pointing to Job as one whom Satan had not been able to pervert. This fact alone, of Job's faithfulness, appears to be enough to enrage the Adversary, who then sought to make Job unfaithful. But by claiming that Job would stay faithful, God refuted the accusations that Satan made against Job—and indirectly against God Himself! If Job would love God, no matter the tragedy that befell him, then obviously Job must have been convinced of God's goodness after all. Apparently, this one faithful person was enough to help prove the Adversary wrong, which is why this evil extraterrestrial worked so mercilessly to make Job turn against God.

Wherever the battle between God and the Adversary

began, and whatever caused it (the book of Job does not say), it was now being fought, not amid the galaxies of the cosmos, but on earth, even more precisely, in the human conscience. Humans, whether they know it or not, realize it or not, or even care or not, are in a cosmic war whose consequences extend far beyond the confines of our little planet.

And though he had no idea of the real issues, Job fought on the front lines. He refuted the Adversary's accusations against himself and, ultimately, God—even if he had no conception of the bigger stakes around him. The story gives no indication that Job knew what transpired in those cosmic scenes. He didn't need to. All he needed to know was God, and what God required of him.

Job's response to the tragedies also gives us insight into the conflict. The story started out mentioning Job's family, his seven sons and three daughters. It then listed his material wealth: the oxen, the sheep, the camels, and the servants, etc. The Adversary, attempting to undermine Job's faith, went after those elements specifically mentioned: the oxen, sheep, camels, servants, and children—the things that helped define Job and mold his identity.

Yet, when tragedy struck, instead of doing what Satan said ("he will curse thee to thy face"), "Job arose, and rent his mantle, and shaved his head, and fell down upon the ground, and worshipped. And said, Naked came I out of my mother's womb, and naked shall I return thither: the Lord gave, and the Lord hath taken away; blessed be the name of the Lord. In all this Job sinned not, nor charged God foolishly" (Job 1:20-22).

When that attack failed, this evil extraterrestrial, rather than trying to undermine Job indirectly, went after Job himself. He smote him with boils, and then used Job's wife to push him over the line. "Curse God," she said, "and die."

"Thou speakest as one of the foolish women speaketh," Job responded. "What? shall we receive good at the hand of God, and shall we not receive evil?" The Bible then says, "In all this did not Job sin with his lips" (Job 2:10).

No question Job suffered. The story wails with bitterness and pain. Almost every word spewed from his mouth was punctuated with cries. "Let the day perish wherein I was born," he moaned, the first words of his speeches, "and the night in which it was said, There is a man child conceived. Let that day be darkness" (Job 3:3, 4).

Though grieving over the tragedies, Job determined to maintain his fidelity, although he didn't understand what was happening, why, or who caused it. "As God liveth, who hath taken away my judgment; and the Almighty, who hath vexed my soul; All the while my breath is in me, and the spirit of God is in my nostrils; my lips shall not speak wickedness, nor my tongue utter deceit. God forbid that I should justify you: till I die I will not remove mine integrity from me. My righteousness I hold fast, and will not let it go: My heart shall not reproach me so long as I live" (Job 27:2-6).

This element of faithfulness remains crucial in understanding the battle between God and the Adversary, and man's role in it. Though much is not revealed in the book of Job, one point is: Satan made accusations—and Job, by staying faithful, showed them to be false!

In the midst of the dialogue, one of Job's friends challenged him: "Is it any pleasure to the Almighty, that thou art righteous? or is it gain to him, that thou makest thy ways perfect?" (Job 22:3). As those cosmic scenes have shown—yes, it is gain to Him!

After Job's family and possessions were taken away, the Bible said that "Job sinned not" (Job 1:22); then, after Job was afflicted, it said that Job did "not sin with his lips" (Job 2:10). These texts don't mean that Job was a sinless being; instead, they show that despite tragedy,

Job did not sin in response to them.

This point, of his not sinning, is repeated purposely. "Sin," the Bible says, "is transgression of the law" (1 John 3:4); it says, too, that "whoever keeps the whole law and yet stumbles at just one point is guilty of breaking all of it" (James 2:10, NIV). Job, however, despite all the trials, didn't break any of the commandments contained in God's law, for the story specifies, twice, that Job didn't sin.

Job knew God's law because, as shown earlier, he obeyed its precepts. The Adversary, by trying to get him to curse God, would have caused Job to break that law, specifically the commandment that forbids taking the name of the Lord in vain, and thus, according to the Bible, Job would have broken them all.

If God's character were under attack, then His law probably would be too, for the law is a transcript of that character. A vicious, arbitrary king makes vicious, arbitrary laws; a gentle, fair ruler makes gentle, fair laws. Hitler's character, for example, was revealed by the government he formed and the laws he used to run it. If God's character were assaulted, His law, which reveals that character, probably would be too. The book of Job, in a roundabout way, by twice mentioning that Job refused to break that law, gives evidence that it was.

The first two chapters of the book show that Job didn't break God's law, even though the Adversary tried to make him, for if God's character were under attack, and God's law reflects that character, then a way to attack God would be to disparage His law. The Adversary, therefore, tried to get Job to break it. Perhaps, by getting Job to sin, he could attack God by asserting that, given the right circumstances, even his holiest followers will transgress the law. If God is so good, so just, so holy, His law would be good, holy, and just as well. Yet if "holy Job" breaks the law, then perhaps that law might not be so good after all, which means that perhaps even God Himself isn't so good either.

Had Job sinned, the Adversary would have triumphed. Instead, Job apparently felt that God was so good, His law so just, that he would obey and stay faithful anyway. Despite the tragedies, the suffering, and the mindless violence against him and his family, Job proved that he loved God so much that he would remain steadfast regardless of the circumstance.

"Though he slay me," Job cried out, "yet will I trust in him" (Job 13:15).

Again, all these events happened before the onlooking "sons of God." By not sinning, by staying faithful, Job showed these other celestial intelligences that the Adversary's accusations against himself, and indirectly God, were hollow lies.

Of course, the book of Job cannot mean that all suffering comes as a cosmic test to see whether or not man will stay faithful, or keep God's law. Millions of children who have died of disease or war haven't had any chance to take sides: they don't know anything about the Adversary, God, or His law. What about the untold masses who never heard of God, who never had a chance to learn of His law? Their sufferings could no more be a test as to whether or not they would stay faithful and not sin than it could be a test for the retarded or the insane, who couldn't comprehend these concepts even if presented to them, any more than it was a test for Job's children, who were crushed by the walls of a house early in the story.

Instead, Job reveals the idea, the principle, that in the midst of all human suffering, some people will stay faithful to God, will keep His law, thus helping to refute the charges brought against God in this great controversy with His cosmic enemy. Not all suffering comes as a test, but suffering does give the opportunity to respond in such a manner that, in the right context, people can bring glory to God and refute the Adversary's accusations before the onlooking universe, even if those involved in the suffering have no conception of the higher issues at stake!

God, in confronting the charges of His accuser, is using man to help answer those charges. Until this point is understood, we can't comprehend why an all-powerful God would allow sin and the suffering it inevitably brings. Once understood, this point neutralizes some (but not all) of the tensions for those who believe in a loving God but can't reconcile that belief with human suffering.

It's easy, from our limited perspective, to ask, "Why doesn't God just end the evil? If there is an evil being who is wreaking havoc on the earth, why doesn't God simply destroy him?" Yet, locked within our limited dimensions of time and space, unable to grasp the whole picture, not seeing what transpires in other parts of the universe, we don't understand that the issues of pain and suffering go far beyond the earth. In Job we begin to see that the issues of good and evil involve not just man, but other intelligences in the universe as well.

This concept is hard for us to comprehend. Despite all our sophisticated computers and powerful rockets, we haven't hurled ourselves any farther out in space than the moon. It's a little like trying to study the bottom of the sea without penetrating an inch below the surface. Because the issues concerning good and evil are ultimately universal and infinite, we are stuck with only our finite minds to comprehend universal and infinite things. At most, we can grasp a minuscule fraction of the whole. Wanting the world, we are like men who clasp in their fingers only handfuls of dirt. As big as the universe is compared to the earth, that's how big the issues of evil and suffering are compared to our conception of them!

For this reason, then, we find it difficult to reconcile a loving, powerful God with human suffering. Some, like

Camus, question the notion of God; others, like Kushner, dilute God until He becomes a semi-impotent deity reduced to the level of a Greek god or goddess.

If, however, Kushner had read the book of Job literally, he would have seen that God has not yet eradicated evil, not because He isn't able, but because He is dealing with it in the context of the whole universe, and therefore it can't be ended until certain universal questions are resolved. The restraints on God are not physical, as Kushner suggested, but are moral.

When a parent puts sharp medicine on a child's wound, the child can't understand why the parent hurts him even more. As humans, we can't begin to understand all the issues involved in this cosmic conflict. We can't understand why God allows evil to continue any more than the child understands why his parent burns him with the medicine, any more than Job or his wife or his friends understood the bigger issues that revolved around them.

"I was the parent of a handicapped child for fourteen years until his death," wrote Rabbi Kushner. "I was not comforted by the notion that God had singled me out because He recognized some special spiritual strength within me and knew that I would be able to handle it better. It didn't make me feel 'privileged.' "

No doubt, too, that, as he sat among the ashes, open sores dripping, perhaps the stench of dead children lingering in his nose—Job would have preferred that God not pointed to him when He confronted Satan in heaven. No doubt, had he had the choice, he would have cried, "Please, God, don't get me involved in this! Use someone else! Give me back my family, my children, my possessions! I can't take it!" Though no one knows why Aaron Kushner died of progeria, no reason would have been acceptable to his father, and, no doubt, given an opportunity, Rabbi Kushner would have pleaded for the life of his son no matter how big the cosmic issues!

When the pain becomes unbearable, when we hurt beyond repair, wouldn't we all choose not to be involved in controversy that began in some distant corner of the universe before we were born, rather than suffer the things we do because of that conflict?

Yet the only choice we have is not whether to be involved (we already are) but whose side we will take.

If, however, we accept this notion of a war between God and the Adversary, a conflict that began in the universe but is battled on earth, one crucial question remains, and until it is answered, this whole "great controversy" approach, taken from the book of Job, quite frankly—stinks.

And that question is: What kind of God would remain in the bliss of heaven, having us poor wretches fight out His battles here on earth?

CHAPTER
Six

How Dare You Judge Us, God!

Spit out of their graves, billions of the world's dead assemble into a quivering sweep of flesh that wraps around the horizon and disappears. Sumerian generals, Celtic merchants, Tibetan mystics, Colombian peasants, Wall Street sceptics—an immeasurable mass, a majority of all who have ever lived upon the earth, rise together, resurrected. The great judgment day has come, and unredeemed humanity stands before the bar of heaven. The crime: high treason against the Law of God. The verdict: guilty as charged. The sentence: eternal destruction.

The condemned don't accept the decree lightly. Cries, curses, accusations surge from their lips, and they rage like an insane sea of boiling flesh.

"How dare You judge me, God!" a man with cropped blond hair shouts, raising a red fist. "What do You know about suffering? What do You know about pain?"

"Sure, I stole," another declares, "but I was hungry. What do You know about hunger, God?"

In the midst of the madness, a woman with painted eyes, a purple tear dripping down her cheek, is thrust on the shoulders of men who greedily handle her.

"What do You know about lust, God?" she accuses. "What do You know about temptation and passion? And yet You are going to sit in heaven and condemn me? We can't stop You! We can't escape, but we reject Your verdict, we reject Your sentence, and we reject You!"

They stomp feet and shake fists as waves of anger rise in hot currents, carrying their cries skyward: "HYPO-CRITE! UNFAIR! HOW EASY IT IS TO BE GOOD IN HEAVEN! HOW DARE YOU JUDGE US!"

A Chinese man, dressed in black, drops his shirt and exposes a back gashed with deep gray scars. He says nothing, then straightens up and shakes a fist over his head while those in the crowd point to his scars and roar: "HOW DARE YOU JUDGE US, GOD!"

"I was arrested unjustly," another man, stepping forward, barks. "I was jailed, beaten, executed. And now, from the comfort of heaven, You condemn me to death— again?"

Amid the madness, each one defies God's right to judge them. A Jew shows the burns on his face from the Zyklon B in a Nazi gas chamber. A Black exposes the scars on his wrists from weeks in chains on a slave ship. Others, rejected by their own society, question whether God, who never knew the pain of rejection, has the right to judge those who have. Political prisoners, who had spoken out for freedom, for truth, and who stood up against tyranny at the cost of their lives, deny God the prerogative to judge them. Though each complaint is different, the consistent cry of this macabre chorus is: "HOW DARE YOU JUDGE US, GOD!"

In a story about the Vietnam War, a G.I. tells about an officer whom the grunts nicknamed Lieutenant

Gladly because he always said to his soldiers, "I wouldn't ask you to do anything that I wouldn't *gladly* do myself." One time, pinned down by enemy fire, Lieutenant Gladly ordered a grunt to run to the other side of a nearby bridge.

"No way, sir," the soldier demurred.

The lieutenant, having muttered threats under his breath, sprang across the bridge himself, but before he went five yards, machine gun fire exploded and, in the words of the grunt, "He got greased."

Apparently, Lieutenant Gladly meant what he said. He would do anything he asked his soldiers to do. As a result, it cost him his life.

But what about God? Is He like a military leader who never sleeps in a muddy foxhole, never feels the heat of shell fire, never faces whizzing bullets, yet who coldly orders thousands of soldiers into foxholes, shell fire, and the whiz of bullets? If this universal star war is real, if God is battling a cosmic enemy, and if humans are the conscripted grunts in the conflict—what kind of God would draft us to fight in a war that began in another part of creation, while He sits on the sidelines watching?

The book of Job again points to an answer. In the nineteenth chapter, after being chastised by Bildad the Shuhite, Job laments: "My kinsfolk have failed, and my familiar friends have forgotten me. They that dwell in mine house, and my maids, count me for a stranger: I am an alien in their sight. I called my servant, and he gave me no answer. . . . All my inward friends abhorred me, and they whom I loved are turned against me. My bone cleaveth to my skin and to my flesh, and I am escaped with the skin of my teeth" (Job 19:14-21).

Then, after asking his friends to pity him, Job—despite his suffering—expresses hope in the coming Redeemer. "For I know that my Redeemer liveth, and that he shall stand at the latter day upon the earth: and though after my skin worms destroy this body, yet in my flesh shall I see God" (Job 19:25, 26).

If the key to understanding why God allows men to suffer is found in the first two chapters of Job, then the key to understanding those two chapters is found in the Redeemer, the one in whom Job expressed hope—Jesus of Nazareth, for Jesus best answers the questions that Job's suffering has raised about God.

No theme in Job better reveals Jesus than does the theme of God's Creatorship. Near the end of the story, after the cycle of speeches, God manifests Himself to Job. Instead of excusing Himself and apologizing for the tragedies, God declares His own creative and sustaining power in contrast to Job's own limitations and weakness: "Where wast thou when I laid the foundations of the earth?" He asked. "Canst thou bind the sweet influences of Pleiades, or loose the bands of Orion? Canst thou bring forth Mazzaroth in his season? Or canst thou guide Arcturus with his sons?" "Doth the hawk fly by thy wisdom, and stretch her wings toward the south? Doth the eagle mount up at thy command, and make her nest on high?" (Job 38:4, 31, 32; 39:26, 27). In these verses, God identifies Himself as the Creator and Sustainer, not only of the earth, but of the universe. Here God reveals His awesome power.

Indeed, no matter how one believes that the universe came into existence, either by the God depicted in Job, or by blind chance, or by the Nordic deity Thor—however it happened, the creation of these billions and billions of galaxies obviously required awesome energy.

The vastness of the universe alone bears irrefutable proof of the power needed to create it. If our minuscule solar system were the size of Manhattan, the nearest star, Alpha Centauri, would be 5,500 miles away in Jerusalem! At the speed of light, 186,000 miles per second (fast enough to circle the earth seven times in a second), thousands, even millions of years would be needed to reach a majority of the stars in creation.

Not only the distances between the celestial bodies, but their sizes as well reveal the power behind creation. A million earths would fill the sun, and about 60,000 suns would fill the star Antares. One of the stars in our own galaxy, Betelgeuse, is a quarter the size of our entire solar system—while another star, Alpha Herculis, has a circumference twenty-five times larger than the circumference of the earth's revolution around the sun!

Meanwhile, the earth moves in a 595-million mile orbit (multiply 595 million by twenty-five for the circumference of Alpha Herculis!) at about eight times the speed of a bullet. Also, the earth spins on its axis at about 1,000 miles an hour and circles the center of the galaxy at about 170 miles per second.

Now, imagine the energy needed to start our "little" earth (25,000 miles in circumference and weighing untold tons) turning on its axis at about a 1,000 miles per hour, much less the power that catapulted it around the sun at eight times the speed of a bullet. And this is just one small planet! Billions upon billions of galaxies, each containing billions of stars, many of which could swallow the sun, which could swallow a million earths—all cruise across the cosmos at incredible speeds. We can no more comprehend the energy involved in the creation of the universe any more than someone whose only known mode of transportation had four legs and ate hay could comprehend supersonic speed.

And though the Bible doesn't detail the creation process, it does detail the Creator. "For by him were all things created," says the Bible about Jesus, "that are in heaven, and that are in earth, visible and invisible, whether they be thrones, or dominions, or principalities, or powers: all things were created by him, and for him. And he is before all things, and by him all

65

things consist" (Colossians 1:16, 17).

"All things were made by him [Jesus]; and without him was not any thing made that was made" (John 1:3).

Jesus was the Creator and Sustainer, the One who can "bind the sweet influences of the Pleiades," and "loose the bands of Orion." He had power that not only created the earth, the sun, Betelgeuse, Antares, and billions and billions of other heavenly bodies, but sent them barnstorming through infinity at breakneck speed as well.

Both the books of John and Colossians stress that "all things" were created by Jesus. And not only did He create all things, from the supernova to the firefly, but He sustains them all as well, for Scripture says that "by him all things consist."

While Scripture clearly depicts Jesus as the Creator, it depicts another aspect of Him as well. "And Jacob the father of Joseph the husband of Mary, of whom Jesus was born, who is called Christ" (Matthew 1:16, RSV).

Imagine! The Creator of the universe, the power that sent Belegeuse, Antares, and billions of galaxies hurling through space, the power that made oceans, air, and elephants—He *shrank* into a helpless human baby?

Forget Tammy Bakker's air-conditioned doghouse, Jimmy Swaggart's hookers, or the sordid history of Christianity. What's important is Jesus, and the essence of Jesus is that even though He was God, the Creator of the universe—He humiliated Himself to become a human being!

Doctrine, liturgy, history, everything is dwarfed by the fact that Creator of the universe, the Commander-in-Chief, voluntarily left the comfort and safety of heaven and became a front-line grunt. God didn't sit by idly while we were decimated by Satan. Who Jesus was and what He did proves that Jesus not only took the brunt of the assault, in a way that no man ever will, but He won

66

the war—a victory in which He has promised to share with us!

And in order for us to enjoy the spoils of Jesus' victory, God had to perfectly identify with humanity, which is why He became a human being. The miracle is not so much the metaphysics of the incarnation. The Being that could speak the earth into existence certainly possessed the power to transform Himself into a human if He wanted. The marvel is not so much how He did it, but that He chose to!

When Jesus, the Creator, was incarnated into His creation, when He "beamed down" into humanity, He wasn't born in a first-class hospital with attending nurses and doctors, as was little William Arthur Philip Louis, H.R.H. Prince William, the future King of England. Instead, this King, the King of the universe, entered the world in a barn.

"And she brought forth her firstborn son, and wrapped him in swaddling clothes, and laid him in a manger; because there was no room for them in the inn" (Luke 2:7).

No room for them? For any other king, they would have emptied the inn; for this one, they didn't even have a bed. The Creator of the universe, who made the fragrance of lilacs, inhaled His first breath amid the stench of animal dung.

Also, unlike Prince William, whose birth was announced to the world, this monarch's entry was unknown except for a few shepherds and wise men who asked, "Where is he that is born King of the Jews?" (Matthew 2:2).

And yet even if Jesus had come to earth as Prince William of England, with all the glamor, glory, and adoration that comes with the post, it still would have been an infinite condescension. Instead, in all the possible times (why not during all the comforts of the

67

twentieth century?), of all the possible places (why not an island paradise?), in all the possible roles (why not the pampered child of a multimillionaire?)—He entered humanity as the offspring of Jewish indigents living more than 1,900 years ago in the ancient Middle East. He purposely became the child of people so poor that when they brought the infant to the temple in Jerusalem to be dedicated to the Lord, they offered a pair of turtledoves or pigeons (instead of the customary lamb), the only offering that these impoverished Jewish peasants from Galilee could afford!

Though He was God, in His new role His mother had become His first human teacher. From her lips, and from the scrolls of the prophets, He learned the spiritual truths that He had taught to ancient Israel centuries before. The words which He had spoken to the nation amid the fire and lightning of Mount Sinai, He now learned at His mother's knee. The God who revealed to Job His own creative majesty and splendor was now dependent upon His mother to read to Him that which He Himself had inspired!

If, however, Jesus became a human being, even starting out as a helpless infant all in order to share the human experience fully—how did He, after His ministry began thirty years after His birth, raise the dead, restore sight to the blind, turn water into wine, and do all His other miracles?

Christ's own words give the answer. While still a child, when visiting the temple in Jerusalem, Jesus had said to his earthly parents: "[Know] ye not that I must be about my Father's business?" (Luke 2:49). He later talked about His Father as "the one who sent me." One of His last prayers on earth was: "O my Father, if it be possible, let this cup pass from me: nevertheless not as I will, but as thou wilt" (Matthew 26:39). Throughout the entire record of His earthly life, Jesus repeatedly spoke of His "heavenly Father" as the one to whom He was submitted.

These words bring in the concept of biblical monotheism. Christians believe in one God composed of three distinct parts, Father, Son, and Holy Spirit, in the same way one dollar can be divided into four complete parts, or quarters. Though the Bible teaches that "God is one," the Hebrew word used here for "one," *'echad,* suggests in other places in the Bible a unity. In the verse, "And there was an evening, and there was a morning, one [*'echad*] day," dealing with Creation, the word for "one" means a whole day composed of two parts—an evening and a morning. The Bible says too that "a man shall leave his father and mother, and shall cleave unto his wife, and they shall become one [*'echad*] flesh." *One* flesh composed of two parts, a man and his wife. One of the greatest Jewish scholars, Maimonides, a monotheist, wrote centuries ago: "I believe with perfect faith that the Creator, blessed be His name, is Unity, and that there is no unity in any manner like unto His, and that He alone is our God who was, is and will be. Hear O Israel, YHWH, Elohenu, YHWH, is one. How can the three names be one? . . . Three modes yet from one Unity."

Though much about this idea of Triune God is not understood, the most important point is: Jesus was fully God, equal with the Father since eternity. When He came to earth, however, Jesus came as a human being and purposely placed Himself in a subordinate role to the Father. Though Jesus was fully God and fully man simultaneously, while on earth He set aside His divine power and submitted Himself as a human being to the Father, who then performed these miracles through Him. Jesus did no miracles through His own power, the power He still possessed as God. Instead, as a human being, He relied only on that power which the Father manifested in Him, and through this power He performed His wonderful works: "For the works which the Father has granted me to accomplish," Jesus said (John 5:36, RSV), "these very works which I am doing, bear me witness that the Father has sent me."

And Jesus not only did the works that He was "granted to accomplish," He also remained obedient and submissive to the prompting of the Divine Spirit as well, no matter where it led Him.

"Then was Jesus led up of the Spirit into the wilderness to be tempted of the devil. And when he had fasted forty days and forty nights, he was afterward an hungered" (Matthew 4:1, 2).

Though He squeezed grainy fields of wheat out of the earth, soaked the peach in tangy juice, and covered the nut in a shell—Jesus Himself starved. His stomach growled, His hands quivered, and His flesh evaporated off his bones. Jesus, the Creator of all food, went without any for forty days!

Then as Jesus languished, Satan appeared. Now, however, this evil extraterrestrial didn't confront the Creator amid the majesty and grandeur in heaven, as he had done in the story of Job. Instead, he challenged God on the earth, on Satan's own turf. Amazed as he must have been to see God, with all His power and glory, transformed into a simple human being, he must have been thrilled at the opportunity to lead Him into sin. God had become part of humanity; Satan had controlled humanity for thousands of years; Jesus, half-dead already, should have been easy prey.

"And when the tempter came to him, he said, If thou be the Son of God, command that these stones be made bread. But he answered and said, It is written, Man shall not live by bread alone, but by every word that proceedeth out of the mouth of God" (Matthew 4:3, 4).

When that approach didn't work, he tried another: "Then the devil taketh him up into the holy city, and setteth him on a pinnacle of the temple, and saith unto him, If thou be the Son of God, cast thyself down: for it is written, He shall give his angels charge concerning thee: and in their hands they shall bear thee up, lest at any time thou dash thy foot against a stone. Jesus said unto him, It is written again, Thou shalt not tempt the Lord thy God" (Matthew 4:5-7).

Satan tried once more: "Again the devil taketh him up into an exceeding high mountain, and sheweth him all the kingdoms of the world, and the glory of them; and saith unto Him, All these things will I give unto thee, if thou wilt fall down and worship me. Then Jesus saith unto Him, Get thee hence, Satan: for it is written, Thou shalt worship the Lord thy God, and him only shalt thou serve. Then the devil leaveth him" (Matthew 4: 8-11).

Here the Adversary tempted Jesus when Jesus was weakened and emaciated in a barren wilderness, a sharp contrast to the temptation of Adam and Eve, who were thriving in a luxurious paradise when enticed. Adam and Eve, their bellies filled in the cool of a garden, succumbed to appetite; Jesus, His belly hollow in the heat of the desert, didn't.

However you view the Eden story, one point is paramount: God did not bring sin to the earth. The Adversary brought it, but only through the fall of Adam and Eve, who, despite clear warnings, disobeyed the Lord and succumbed to appetite. Therefore, because man obeyed his word over God's, the Adversary claimed the earth as his own, with thousands of years of human suffering as the consequence.

Jesus, however, came to win the earth back. By coming as a man and resisting temptations worse than any man will face, Jesus proved that men didn't need to sin. Because Jesus came in the same flesh as humanity, and obeyed God's law in that flesh, He proved that man too can obey that law, and He did it without using His own

71

power. Instead, He was completely dependent on the power of the Father, thus setting an example how humans are to be dependent upon and submissive to God in order to obtain victory over sin as well, the same way Job also resisted. Jesus obeyed the law the same way men are to obey: through submission to divine power.

Satan's first temptation, therefore, was to lure Jesus into transforming rocks into bread. If Jesus, using His own Divinity, had turned those stones into grain, the Adversary would have triumphed because Jesus could no longer be man's example. Had Jesus, hungry as He was, used His own power in order to provide for Himself, the plan of salvation would have been broken. Why? Because, in order for the plan of salvation to be efficacious, Jesus had to come as a man, with no unfair advantages, to prove that man, in submission to divine power, could obey God. Otherwise, Adam and Eve's original fall could be blamed on God, for asking them to do something that they could not do and then punishing them for not doing it. If Jesus, in a barren wilderness, could stay faithful, then Adam and Eve, in a lush garden, should have too.

The same principle holds true with men. Why would God make a law that we can't keep, and then punish us for not keeping it? The answer, of course, is that He didn't. Jesus, by His sinless life, proved that man can keep God's law; therefore, sin, which is transgression of that law, is man's fault, not God's.

And, as the story of Job revealed, obedience to God's law is a crucial factor in the conflict with Satan. In this battle in the wilderness, Satan tried to get Jesus to break that law by tempting Him, in His weakened state, to worship him instead of the Lord. As part of the lure, he promised to give Jesus all the kingdoms of the world, but Jesus resisted the temptation to break the commandment that forbade worshiping any god but the Lord: "Thou shalt have no other gods before me."

72

Here, too, as in Job, the issue was worship: would Jesus worship the true God despite great pressure not to? Jesus, like Job, refused to submit to the Adversary's temptations, and, here too, as with Job, God won.

Jesus' sufferings, however, weren't limited to the wilderness. "His life had been one of persecution and insult. Driven from Bethlehem by a jealous king, rejected by His own people at Nazareth, condemned to death without a cause at Jerusalem. . . . He who was ever touched by human woe, who healed the sick, restored sight to the blind, hearing to the deaf, and speech to the dumb, who fed the hungry and comforted the sorrowful, was driven from the people He had labored to save. He who walked upon the heaving billows, and by a word silenced their angry roaring, who cast out devils that in departing acknowledged Him to be the Son of God, who broke the slumbers of the dead, who held thousands entranced by His words of wisdom, was unable to reach the hearts of those who were blinded by prejudice and hatred, and who stubbornly rejected the light" (Ellen G. White, *The Desire of Ages,* Pacific Press, p. 541).

Jesus, the One who gave mankind the law, was accused of breaking that law. Jesus, the One who came to the earth to defeat and break the devil's hold on the earth, was accused of being the devil. Jesus, who came "to the lost sheep of the house of Israel," was rejected by those sheep. Jesus, who came to reveal to men about God, was charged with blaspheming God. Jesus, who traveled across the universe to the earth in order to give men life, faced a mob that tried to kill Him by throwing Him off a cliff.

"Foxes have holes," Jesus said after the turmoil in the wilderness, "and birds of the air have nests, but the Son of man hath not where to lay his head" (Luke 9:58).

Though He created the wood, stone, and metals used to build homes, He now had no home of His own, not even a place to sleep. At the end of His earthly ministry, after three and a half years of toil, much of the time misunderstood and rejected, Jesus, having eaten His last meal with His disciples, "laid aside his garments; and took a towel, and girded himself. After that he poureth water into a bason, and began to wash the disciples' feet and to wipe them with the towel" (John 13:4, 5).

Though He was God, one of His last acts on earth was to wash the feet of those who should have been at His feet, washing and worshiping Him.

Later, in the garden of Gethsemane, His enemies came and "the band and the captain and officers of the Jews took Jesus, and bound him" (John 18:12).

He—who could free the blind from darkness, release the sinner from sin, and liberate the dead from the grave—allowed Himself to be taken captive.

When Jesus spoke before the high priest, "one of the officers which stood by struck Jesus with the palm of his hand, saying, Answerest thou the high priest so?" (John 18:22).

Jesus, from whose mouth sprang the words that created the earth, was struck on that mouth by one of His own creatures.

"Then Pilate therefore took Jesus, and scourged him. And the soldiers platted a crown of thorns, and put it on his head, and they put on him a purple robe. And said, Hail, King of the Jews! and they smote him with their hands" (John 19:1-3).

He, who for endless ages had listened to the adoration and praise from the creatures of the worlds that He had created, now submitted Himself to taunts and jeers from ignorant men.

"And he bearing his cross went forth into a place called the place of a skull, which is called in the Hebrew Golgotha" (John 19:17).

The One who sustained the universe now carried a

cross on His bleeding back!

"And they crucified him" (Matthew 27:35).

God allowed men to drive spikes into the flesh of His hands and feet, and then to hang Him by those spikes on a cross!

"And they that passed by reviled him, wagging their heads, and saying, . . . If thou be the Son of God, come down from the cross. Likewise also the chief priests mocking him, with the scribes and elders, said, He saved others; himself he cannot save. If he be the King of Israel, let him now come down from the cross, and we will believe him. He trusted in God; let him deliver him now, if he will have him: for he said, I am the Son of God" (Matthew 27:39-43).

He, who could have come down and annihilated these mockers, instead hung there in order to save them.

"And at the ninth hour Jesus cried with a loud voice, saying, Eloi, Eloi, lama sabachthani? which is, being interpreted, My God, my God, why hast thou forsaken me? (Mark 15:34).

Jesus, who had been one with the Father from eternity, now felt the separation from God that sin brings as the concentrated guilt of all the world's sin crushed out His existence.

"And Jesus cried with a loud voice, and gave up the ghost" (Mark 15:37).

Jesus, the Source of all life, allowed His own life to be ended by the sins of a world that would mostly reject Him anyway!

"How dare You judge us, God?" the mob, stretched across the horizon, screams. "How dare You? What do You know about pain, what do You know about suffering, what do You know about death? And You, You are going to judge us?"

A flash of light explodes over them. All shadows,

75

colors, everything for a blinding moment are bleached white. The billions freeze, their accusations locked inside open jaws.

They stare upward. They see the figure of Jesus, whose poverty, hunger, toil, temptation, suffering, and humiliation is graphically portrayed across the sky. They watch Him, a human being, fiercely tempted, yet not overcome. They see Him preach truth, and stand for righteousness, as no man had ever done, and they see Him, rejected, hated, and arrested for it. They see Him, the only sinless, innocent man, beaten, tortured, humiliated and killed in the prime of His life—and all because of their sins.

All of them, from savages to priests, from prisoners to kings—comparing His life with theirs—realize their own wretchedness, sin, and evil in contrast to Jesus. Overwhelmed with guilt, they want to cover their eyes and turn away from the images played before them, but it is impossible.

A hollow silence settles over the crowd. No more fingers point, no more feet stomp, no more accusations ring out, and no more is the question, How dare You judge us, God? hurled toward heaven.

They now know.

CHAPTER

Seven

The Unreasonable Silence

No one can grasp what it meant for the Creator to become a man, because no one can grasp creation. It is like trying to compare the size of a man to the universe: we can't, because the size of the universe is beyond human comprehension—and if we can't comprehend the creation, then how can we comprehend the Creator? Therefore we don't begin to understand how much of a condescension it was for God to incarnate into humanity.

We can, however, understand the implications of that incarnation—and they are staggering. God has so closely associated Himself with us, our pain, disappointments, fears, and sorrows that no one can justly accuse Him of indifference to our plight. On the contrary, through Jesus, God has linked Himself to us with bonds that can never be broken.

Even writer Albert Camus, in one of his less rebellious moments, understood the significance of Jesus Christ's relationship to humanity, though apparently he never accepted it for himself.

"The Christ came to solve two principal problems, evil and death," he wrote in *The Rebel,* "which are essentially the problem of rebels. His solution consisted first of all in taking on their condition. The God-man suffers also— with patience. Evil and death are no longer absolutely imputable to him inasmuch as he suffers and dies. The night on Golgotha has so great an importance in the history of men only because the divinity, ostensibly abandoning its traditional privileges, lived through to the end the anguish of death and of despair."

Yet Jesus, by suffering with us, did much more than link Himself with humanity. Through transgression, man separated himself from God, and thus Jesus came to bring them back together. First, by living without sin, He possessed a perfect character, the only character worthy of the eternal life that God had originally wanted to bestow upon man at creation. Second, Jesus offered His perfect life to pay the penalty for all the sins that men have or ever would commit, the sins that have brought about this painful split between heaven and earth. "And all things are of God, who hath reconciled us to himself by Jesus Christ . . . that God was in Christ, reconciling the world unto himself, not imputing their trespasses unto them" (2 Corinthians 5:18, 19).

Therefore, the moment a person accepts that at the cross Jesus paid for their sins Himself, and then surrenders himself to Jesus as a result of that acceptance, he is forgiven those sins, and the perfect life of Jesus is then credited to him as his own. From that moment on, when God looks upon that person, instead of seeing a sinner whose iniquities have separated him from God, He sees the perfection of Jesus, which covers the converted sinner like a robe. Thus man and God are reunited through Jesus.

This imputation of Christ's righteousness to us forms

the basis of the gospel message. What Jesus did for us, in place of us, outside of us 2,000 years ago at Calvary, can assure us of eternal life now! "There is therefore now no condemnation to them which are in Christ Jesus" (Romans 8:1).

Job had that assurance too. While today we look back to the cross for the assurance of salvation, Job offered animal sacrifices that pointed him forward to it. The purpose of the ancient sacrificial system, as given by God, was to reveal the atoning death of Jesus for all humanity. Each beast, sacrificed for the sins of the individual sinner, symbolized Jesus, who would be sacrificed for the sins of the world. "But God commendeth his love toward us, in that, while we were yet sinners, Christ died for us" (Romans 5:8).

How much Job understood of the plan of salvation depicted in those sacrifices the story does not say. But, despite having his family killed, his possessions destroyed, and his flesh rotted, Job understood enough about the Redeemer to be assured that, even if his body decayed in death, he would one day be resurrected unto eternal life: "For I know that my Redeemer lives, and at last he will stand upon the earth; and after my skin has been thus destroyed, then from my flesh I shall see God" (Job 19:25, 26, RSV).

The resurrection of the dead? People buried for thousands of years revived to life? Others, their flesh consumed by fire or fish, put back together and given breath? When I first became a believer in Jesus, I knew that belief in God required faith in things I could not see or totally comprehend, but to believe that the billions who have died on the earth—many who now float in the clouds, not as ethereal spirits, but as dust—would someday live again?

One afternoon during my struggle with doubt, I was browsing through an astronomy periodical in a magazine rack. Under pictures of vast galaxies cartwheeling through the cosmos, a caption said that more galaxies exist than humans who have ever lived, and that any one of these galaxies alone contained more stars than there were humans throughout all earth's history.

Instantly, my skepticism about the resurrection vanished. I had no more understanding on how the dead could be raised, any more than I understood how billions of galaxies teeming with stars could be created. Imagining how these galaxies could have been formed seemed as futile to my finite mind as was imagining how the dead could be resurrected. Yet I didn't need much faith to believe that those galaxies existed. I knew that they did.

I realized then that God, who could spin a hundred billion galaxies across the cosmos, could also bring back to life the few billion humans who live on the earth. The Power who made the universe certainly possessed the creative potential to resurrect the dead! If God could create and sustain the cosmos, the resurrection of this tiny planet's dead should be a snap.

What I learned was not how God resurrected the dead—but simply that He could!

But if God did create everything, from galaxies to glowworms, and if He does have the creative power to resurrect the earth's dead, another important question needs answering: Did God create Satan? If so, does the blame for sin and suffering then fall back on God, Satan's creator?

Again, the book of Job has answers.

In trying to understand why bad things happen to good people, Rabbi Harold Kushner wrote about a randomness in the creation, "where God's creative light has not yet penetrated." That concept, we saw, was wrong. The suffering in the world comes not because of God's absence, but, as the book of Job revealed, because of the presence of an intruder who has been defacing the earth and leading men into sin for thousands of years. This concept is revealed in the New Testament as well: "Be sober, be vigilant; because your adversary the devil, as a roaring lion, walketh about, seeking whom he may devour" (1 Peter 5:8).

But from where did the Adversary come? Though the book of Job doesn't say specifically, it does present a theme that helps explain the origin, not only of the Adversary, but of evil itself: the theme of free will.

In the book of Job, Satan used external pressure, both physical and economic, to try to change Job's worship. God, in response, used none. Job had the God-given freedom to succumb to the enemy's wiles. Job could have cursed his Creator, abandoned his faith, even rejected God, as the Adversary tried to make Job do. God was not going to stop Job. Instead, no matter how much pressure the Adversary put on Job, God applied none to counteract it. If Job was going to stay faithful, it would be of his own free will. And Job, so convinced of God's goodness, did stay faithful, anyway. "Though he slay me," Job uttered, "yet will I trust him."

Job's steadfastness came as a result of free choice on his part. Job remained faithful because he loved God, not because God forced him to, and this love produces the only type of faithfulness that God accepts, which is why Jesus said that the most important commandment was to "love the Lord thy God with all thine heart, with all thy soul, and with all thy might." If we love God with all our hearts, we will worship and obey Him out of free choice—the same way Job did, the same way that God wants all His creation to worship and obey Him.

This principle of free choice is not limited to humans. The first few chapters in Job revealed extraterrestrial "sons of God" who witnessed the great controversy between God and the Adversary. God wanted to answer the Adversary's accusations in a way that would show these beings the falsity of the Adversary's charges against

81

Him. If God had forced the allegiance of these other intelligences, then He had no need to answer Satan's charges openly before them. He could have just arbitrarily vaporized him from the start, and these other powers would have had to serve Him anyway.

Instead, God Himself became "a man of sorrows and acquainted with grief," partly to reveal to the universe just how much He would go through to keep their allegiance without violating the sanctity of free will. Had God forced obedience, then He would not have had to suffer and die before the onlooking universe. So sacred did God deem free will, that He Himself went to the cross rather than trample on it.

The Adversary, a created being, also had the choice whether or not to serve God. The story of Job doesn't explain the origin of his antagonisms, but apparently this extraterrestrial, using the God-given prerogative of free will that God has given to all creation, decided to rebel. The book of Ezekiel gives glimpses of Satan as a beautiful and powerful being ("every precious stone was thy covering"), "perfect in thy ways from the day thou wast created" (Ezekiel 28:15). Yet, for some reason, in contrast to Job, he eventually turned against his Creator. God didn't create the nasty, vindictive extraterrestrial depicted in the book of Job; instead, He created a being "full of wisdom, and perfect in beauty" who, exercising the same free will that each human being possesses now, rebelled. Sin, or disobedience, was not God's creation, nor His fault, but He allowed Himself to suffer the penalty for it anyway, taking it all upon Himself at Calvary.

This issue of free choice remains crucial in understanding the human predicament. Most pain and suffering today results from the abuse of free will, the same free will that the Adversary abused somewhere in the cosmos thousands of years ago.

The book of Revelation teaches that this issue of free choice will climax on the earth in the final battle between Christ and the enemy, a battle not fought in some Middle Eastern desert over the sovereignty of Jerusalem, but fought in and over the hearts of men—just as it was in Job. Indeed, Revelation reveals on a massive scale what the book of Job revealed on an individual one.

Though about 1,500 years separate the writing of the books of Job and Revelation, the two books have much in common. Many elements in Job are repeated in Revelation 12-14, chapters that predict a last-day persecution similar to what Job endured.

First, in these chapters in Revelation, as in Job, the Adversary appears, this time symbolized as a dragon: "The great dragon was cast out, that old serpent called the Devil, and Satan, which deceiveth the whole world" (Revelation 12:9).

The theme of God's creatorship, and the worship He claims because of that creatorship, is found in Revelation too: "Worship him who made the heavens, the earth, the sea and the springs of water!" the book of Revelation (14:7, NIV) declares. Here it calls for followers who will, like Job, not only believe in the Creator, but worship Him as well!

Unfortunately, just as Job faced pressure to turn away from this worship, these people depicted in Revelation will also. Chapter 13 warns of a religious-political power, called "the beast," that will use economic and physical coercion to hijack the worship that God alone deserves and divert it to another source, described in Revelation as "the image of the beast." Warning about this power, Revelation says that it causes "all who refused to worship the image to be killed" (Revelation 13:15, NIV).

Beside using physical coercion to attempt to commandeer the worship of God, this power will use economic force as well, as in Job: "He also forced everyone, small and great, rich and poor, free and slave, to receive a mark on his right hand or on his forehead, so that no one could buy or sell unless he had the mark" (verses 16, 17). According to Revelation, only those who worship the image of the beast get this mark (a symbol used to describe these worshipers), which allows them to buy and sell, while those who worship the Creator will face economic sanctions, and the threat of death.

The most important element Job and these people share in common is not persecution, but their steadfastness in it. Job refused to sin despite the pressure against him. Facing tremendous economic and physical harassment, Job worshiped the Creator and kept His commandments. Job's obedience to the law, and His worship of the Creator amid economic and physical coercion, links his experience to the people described in Revelation 12-14, who will worship the Creator and obey His commandments even if, like Job, they face economic and physical pressure not to!

"And the dragon was wroth with the woman [an Old and New Testament symbol for God's people], and went to make war with the remnant of her seed, which keep the commandments of God" (Revelation 12:17).

Referring to Job's stamina amid suffering, James wrote, "Ye have heard of the patience of Job" (James 5:11). Referring to God's faithful people, who will suffer in a similar manner as did Job, Revelation says, "Here is a call for the endurance of the saints, those who keep the commandments of God" (Revelation 14:12, RSV).

Revelation and Job, despite fifteen centuries between them, have parallels. Revelation confronts the large religious and political issues that the worshipers of the Creator will face, while the book of Job presents the conflict as an individual struggle. As in Job, an evil power will use economic and physical coercion to trample upon a right so basic that even God won't tread upon it: the right to worship as one pleases. Revelation teaches also that God will have a people who will endure, a people who, like Job, will worship the Creator and keep His commandments.

In almost no other biblical book is the theme of religious persecution so pervasive as in Job, one of the oldest books (if not the oldest) in the Bible, and as in Revelation, one of the newest (if not the newest). Maybe God sandwiched almost everything else between them in order to show that from the earliest times, the time of Job—to the end of time, the time of Revelation 12-14, God's faithful followers, those who worship the Creator and keep His commandments, should be prepared to face persecution for doing so.

Yet even if religious persecution has caused suffering in the past, and according to the book of Revelation will cause more again—for most people now, religious persecution is not the problem. Instead, fear, alienation, poverty, disease, violence, and loneliness are accomplishing in them what Satan accomplished in Job, often worse.

Children are daily being beaten, abandoned, and abused, their cries staining the air in tiny daubs of pain. While someone sits comfortably, stomach full, and reads these words—someone else, living in a alley, belly hollow as a drum, crouches like an animal in a cardboard box. Before a reader turns this page, someone wanting to live will die, while another wanting to die, lives. Parents weep over the graves of their children, children weep over the graves of their parents, and some dead have none to weep over them at all. From space the earth glistens like a blue-and-white gem; up close, it darkens like a boil on Job's skin.

Indeed, even if one accepts this whole great controversy scenario—an evil extraterrestrial, the God-man Jesus, Job, Eden, a cosmic war, everything—many things still don't make sense, still don't fit the formula we find etched out in the biblical story of Job.

Describing a typical day at Auschwitz, Holocaust survivor Elie Wiesel wrote, "Women carrying children were sent with them to the crematorium. Children were of no labor value so they were killed. . . . When the extermination of the Jews in the gas chamber was at its height, orders were issued that children were to be thrown straight into the crematorium furnaces, or into a pit near the crematorium, without being gassed first."

Though this barbarity bears the fingerprints of the evil extraterrestrial, what higher purpose was accomplished? What could the children have possibly learned? And even if they learned something, what good did it do them when dead? And even if Elie Wiesel learned something by witnessing this tragedy that made him a better man, even if it caused him to be more faithful to God, the price couldn't possibly be worth it.

When Pan Am flight 103 was blown out of the Scottish sky by terrorists, and hundreds crashed to a fiery death, could all their families have been ready to meet tragedy, as was Job? Did God, who knows the beginning from the end, specifically select these few hundred people and place them on this flight, knowing that when it went down, their specific families would then have an opportunity to respond to tragedy in the same manner as did Job, thus helping refute before the onlooking universe the devil's accusations against Him? Not likely.

Some things, even with this cosmic perspective, don't add up. Parents, even Christian parents, pray until they're hoarse for a sick child to heal, but the child dies—while another person thanks God for answering her prayer that the washing machine be fixed.

Why are some prayers so miraculously answered, while others seem unheeded? In the religious strife of seventeenth-century England, a Christian, pursued by enemies, hid inside a kiln in an old malt house. As he prayed for deliverance, a spider wove a web across the entrance of the kiln. As the web was finished, his enemies entered the malt house, but as they approached the kiln, they saw the web and stopped.

"No sense to look in there," a pursuer said. "See that web. He couldn't have hid in there without breaking it." They left, and he escaped.

But what about the prayers of Christian John Hooper, who in 1555 was slowly burned at the stake? " 'Lord Jesus, [Hooper cried] have mercy upon me! Lord Jesus receive my spirit!' " And they were the last words he was heard to utter. But when he was black in the mouth, and his tongue so swollen that he could not speak, yet his lips went until they were shrunk to the gums: and he knocked his breast with his hand until one of his arms fell off, and then he knocked still with the other, while fat, water, and blood dripped out at his fingers' ends."

Or who answered Billy Graham's supplication to the Almighty? "I have asked you for a moral and spiritual restoration in the land," this good Christian prayed in the 1960s, "and give thanks that in Thy sovereignty Thou has permitted Richard M. Nixon to lead us at this momentous hour of our history."

The answer again can be found in the book of Job, only now Job doesn't give the answer, which really is the answer itself, namely—that we don't have all the answers.

No matter how much the book of Job revealed by exposing the work, methods, and character of this extraterrestrial intruder, the story of Job still leaves much unexplained. What about Job's seven sons and three daughters crushed under a collapsed house? Did they suffer long under the weight of the house, or were they killed instantly? Either way, what about all their hopes, plans, and dreams? Was it fair for these young people to be killed?

What about Job's servants, who were either burned or disemboweled? After each calamity, one servant escaped.

Four times, a different servant said, "I only am escaped alone to tell thee." Why did those four get away, while the rest were mercilessly murdered?

And what about Job's wife? Those were *her* children, the fruit of *her* womb, dead under the rubble. She saw all the property destroyed, and the servants killed as well. It was her husband who rotted with disease. She probably suffered worse than he, because at least Job maintained his hope and faith in God while she, losing almost everything Job did, lost her faith as well. So hurt, so bitter, she told her husband not only to curse God, but to die. To tell her own husband to die, she must have been deliriously desperate. Why did she have to suffer? Didn't God know that she wouldn't be able to stand the trial? Why did she have to be dragged into this conflict involving God, the Adversary, and Job?

Nowhere does Job himself get an explanation of the tragedies, either. His friends utter quaint clichés about suffering, most of which are wrong, none of which Job accepts: "I have heard many such things: miserable comforters are ye all. Shall vain words have an end? or what emboldeneth thee that thou answerest. I also could speak as ye do: if your soul were in my soul's stead, I could heap up words against you, and shake mine head at you" (Job 16:2-4). Even God, when He appears at the end of the story, offers no explanation to Job for the trials.

Though life eventually turned around for Job—"the Lord gave Job twice as much as he had before"—neither he nor his family ever understood the issues. The last chapter in the book says that after Job's restoration, "all his brethren, and all his sisters, and all they that had been of his acquaintance before . . . comforted him over all the evil that the *Lord* had brought upon him" (Job 42:11). They still blamed God, when the real culprit, working unseen, was the Adversary.

Even when upon the earth, Jesus didn't explain every-thing about evil and good, or about who suffers and why.

"There were present at that season some that told him of the Galileans, whose blood Pilate had mingled with their sacrifices. And Jesus answering said unto them, Suppose ye that these Galileans were sinners above all the Galileans, because they suffered such things? I tell you, Nay: but except ye repent, ye shall also likewise perish. Or those eighteen, upon whom the tower of Siloam fell, and slew them, think ye that they were sinners above all men that dwelt in Jerusalem? I tell you, Nay: but, except ye re-pent, ye shall all likewise perish" (Luke 13:1-5).

Jesus never explained why these tragedies happened, what higher purpose was accomplished, or why some suffered and not others. Those listening to Jesus had no better understanding of what caused these events or why, than did Job or his family about the catastrophes that crushed him.

Even with an understanding of the unseen, as re-vealed in the book of Job, questions remain. But where don't they? No matter one's religion, philosophy, or worldview, no matter if one is an evolutionist, a Marxist, or a geologist—questions remain. We don't understand everything about granite, much less the cosmic battle between good and evil. How can anyone fully compre-hend the moral issues that affect the entire universe, when we have unanswered questions about the rocks beneath our feet?

The book of Job teaches that suffering and evil are part of a cosmic upheaval involving issues and con-sequences that extend beyond earth, into the reaches of creation. What finite human could possibly understand everything involved? Job didn't, we can't—and though we know more than Job, much remains unanswered.

Perhaps the most important message from the book of Job is found not by what it answers about pain and suffering, but by what it *doesn't*. These gaping holes simply show that inexplicable tragedy is part of life, and that this tragedy will not be understood by us now any more than it was understood by Job then. Some questions—such as, why did Aaron Kushner suffer and die of progeria, or why were those on Pan Am flight 103 killed?—are not going to be answered any time soon. The bottom line is, perhaps, that a world suffused with passion, greed, racism, and other sin, will be suffused with suffering, pain, and death as a result. It couldn't be any other way.

What the book of Job does show is that we are involved in a universal struggle between good and evil, the ultimate in star wars, and in this struggle God calls us to worship Him and keep His commandments—as Job did, as God's people in the last days will do (see Revelation 14:12). Though we can't see through the wreckage of our own lives, or the wreckage of the lives of others, somehow, someway, we need to trust God anyway, to believe, as He has so clearly promised, that He can ultimately bring good out of all this evil even if all we know is pain, broken hopes, and disappointment now.

Job himself reveals this principle. As he sat in the ashes, did he ever imagine that the account of his drama would be penned in the most widely read book in history? Had he any idea that for thousands of years, millions of people speaking hundreds of tongues would draw from his tragedy the hope and comfort that would help them through theirs? As he mourned the loss of his children, could he have guessed that over three thousand years later, when men made machines that could fly and sailed boats *under* water, writers at computer terminals would base books on his story?

If, as he sat amid the ashes, he had known how much comfort his calamity would bring to others, would he have thought the price worth it? Probably not. But, apparently, God did, not only for the benefit of those on earth, but for those onlooking "sons of God" as well.

Job is a microcosm, one man's example of almost all men. Though expressed under different circumstances, in different cultures, in different terms, and manifested in almost as many different ways as there are humans, the issue is the same: will our lives prove God or the Adversary right in this great controversy between good (Christ) and evil (Satan)? Whether we consciously choose sides, whether we even know which side we're on, or even if we aren't aware of the conflict, almost all humanity is involved.

The battle for the soul of Job is the same that is raging for the souls of all mankind. By not sinning, by not succumbing, and by remaining faithful to God and keeping His commandments, Job helped prove Satan's accusations wrong before the onlooking universe. How men react to trials, temptations, evil and good, no matter how senseless so much of it seems—determines whom we will help prove right, either God or the enemy, in this cosmic conflict waging before the whole creation!

We are not alone. The universe is watching. "We have been made a spectacle to the whole universe," said the apostle Paul, "to angels as well as to men" (1 Corinthians 4:9, NIV). Our lives, like Job's, can help resolve this conflict, and therefore our joys, sorrows, deeds, words, and every aspect of our existence have a pertinence and importance extending beyond the limited sphere of the earth. Who we are and what we do has consequences that echo throughout the universe!

Were we not crucial, were not what happened to us of paramount concern, then Jesus the Creator of the Universe would not have walked the bloody and bitter path to the cross all in order to rescue us! As big as the universe is compared to human beings, that's how great God's love is for us, for the Creator Himself stepped across that wide gulf between Creator and creation and became a human being.

And because Jesus became a human, He knows our suffering and temptations, and how to help us through them. "Because he himself suffered when he was tempted, he is able to help those who are being tempted" (Hebrews 2:18, NIV). He knows our pain, our sorrows, our suffering because He went through them Himself, only worse—and He holds out His scarred hands to embrace us, to comfort us, to heal our wounds.

No matter who you are, you hurt, you cry, you bleed. Nothing can change that now, not even Christ. Job was so good that God called him "perfect and upright," "the greatest of all the men in the east," yet look what happened to him. Christianity doesn't promise freedom from suffering; on the contrary, it guarantees suffering, but life itself guarantees it too. What Christianity can do is make that suffering more bearable and meaningful, because what Job shows is that through our faith and obedience, pain and misery, though inexplicable to us here and now, can have consequences that reach far beyond what we see or understand ourselves.

"There are two states in which we live," said comedian Woody Allen, "miserable and horrible." Stranded in a world suffused with divorce, cruise missiles, and crack— how could we live any other way? Some just deal with it better than others; some don't deal well with it at all.

And some have Jesus, the crucial difference. He alone can give meaning to our meaningless, purpose to our chaos, and *some* joy for despair, and *some* hope for disappointment. Anything else is as useless as a spoonful of Pepto-Bismol for botulism poisoning. We might be marooned on this dirty, dying stinkhole of a planet, but because of Jesus, we have not been deserted.

No doubt, it was this hope of the Redeemer, as seen through the animal sacrifices, that helped Job remain faithful in his trial. Eventually Job regained his health, received twice as many possessions as before, had ten more children, and lived a long fruitful life. "So the Lord blessed the latter end of Job more than his beginning" (Job 42:12).

Obviously, the writer of the book of Job knew that not everyone's "latter end" is as prosperous as Job's. Most aren't. But if the Bible teaches anything, it teaches that sin and suffering will not last forever. "What do ye imagine against the Lord? he will make an utter end: affliction shall not rise up a second time" (Nahum 1:9). "For, behold, I create new heavens and a new earth: and the former shall not be remembered, nor come into mind" (Isaiah 65:17).

This glimpse of paradise, far from being a fantasy conjured up by an ancient utopian mystic, is simply the promise of the earth recreated the way God originally intended it to be, the way it was before Satan defiled it with sin. Even the promise of eternal life is nothing but the resumption of the life that God originally planned to bestow upon us at creation, the life we lost through transgression of God's law.

And, in this restored life, when the redeemed of God stand robed in a flesh that will never wrinkle, rot, or die, when the veil between the seen and unseen (which the story of Job lifted a little) will be lifted almost all the way—what now appears to be only turmoil, confusion, and heartache will instead be seen as the marvelous providence of God working to ultimately bring good out of evil, no matter how impossible that possibility seems now. Jesus will then clearly answer the questions that stymie us. It will be clear to all that He has refuted the Adversary's charges before the universe. When all the hidden things of darkness are brought to light, when all the secrets of human hearts are shouted across the cosmos, God's faithful people, all creation, even unredeemed humanity—even the enemy himself, will exclaim as Job had thousands of years earlier: "Blessed be the name of the Lord!"

"O taste and see," says Psalm 34:8, "that the Lord is good!" Millions have tasted, and they know—God *is* indeed good. Only by tasting now, by knowing Him and experiencing His mercy and love *personally* can you know the certainty of the hope He holds out before us. For those outside of God looking in, these promises seem no more substantive than daydreams; for those who live by the words of God, who experience them daily, they know that these promises are the prime ingredients of reality. Everything else, the elements of unbelief, humanism, and absurdity are woven from lies and illusions, as deceptive as a magician's wand.

Ultimate reality, ultimate truth, comes from the cross of Calvary. That cross put to death all human philosophy and ideology too. Those nails ripped through not only the flesh of Jesus but through the flimsy tin covers of all manmade belief, exposing the inane, trivial banter of which they are made in relation to the absolute reality of the Creator of the universe dying for the sins of His creation.

Here God Himself hung, and the cry of a father to his children, *Don't you see it, won't you believe it, can't you accept it?* echoes across creation. For those who don't, won't, can't—you're born, you suffer, you die, you rot. Existence becomes absurdity.

"The absurd is born," wrote Albert Camus, "of the confrontation between the human call and the unreasonable silence of the world."

Though Camus had heard the spikes piercing the flesh of divinity, though he heard the men wagging their tongues, and though he heard Jesus crying, "It is finished!" he didn't listen hard enough to understand that those sounds were the answer to that "human call." Thus, for him, the world's "unreasonable silence" continued.

94

We need to surrender to Jesus, we need to give ourselves to Him now. Whether you believe it, accept it, or even want it, Jesus died for your sins. The question is, Will His death for you be in vain?

It doesn't have to be. Dare you have hope amid the misery that surrounds, poisons, and embitters us? Dare you trash all your preconceived notions, opinions, and philosophies, which provide little peace and no promise, for a hope greater than any utopian mystic ever conjured up in his most enraptured visions—the hope which God through Christ offers for those who believe.

"You are a mist," said James (4:14, NIV), "that appears for a little while and then vanishes." What is our miserable, nasty, brutish existence to an eternity without the snags that make it so nasty, miserable and brutish; especially when, one day soon, this earth will be consumed by a purifying fire that will cleanse it of everything that ever had to do with sin, suffering, and death. "And the elements shall melt with fervent heat, the earth also and the works that are therein shall be burned up" (2 Peter 3:10)—and those souls redeemed from the purchase of Christ's blood will inhabit it: "Nevertheless we, according to his promise, look for new heavens and a new earth, wherein dwelleth righteousness" (verse 13).

Soon this great controversy between Christ and the extraterrestrial will end, and the only sign, the only hint that the Adversary ever existed will not be a burned-out tank left to rust in a field, or an empty beer can collecting dead leaves under a bush. Instead, Jesus Himself will carry on His hands and feet the scars from the cross, an eternal testimony to all creation of the unfailing love of God for a world that mostly failed to love Him.

You've read his books.

Now read about the man.

Clifford Goldstein has become one of our most compelling writers. His writing sparkles with vivid imagery and passion. It's hard to believe that this powerful Christian communicator was once a blasphemous agnostic.

Pacific Press invites you to share the drama of Clifford Goldstein's unforgettable autobiographical thriller:

BESTSELLER

Fiery young writer Clifford Goldstein sought fame and fortune in the bestselling novel he was writing. Yet, while pursuing the god of success, he longed for something to believe in.

Bestseller is a story of passions —for glory and for truth. Only one passion would survive the explosive confrontation that takes place when Cliff hurls out the challenge: **"Show your face, God—if you have one —if you dare!"**
US$6.95/Cdn$8.70. Paper, 96 pages.
